THE COUNTER
REFORMATION

THE COUNTER REFORMATION

A. G. DICKENS

Recent Director of the Institute Of Historical Research,
University of London

W · W · NORTON & COMPANY · New York · London

Frontispiece
1 Counter Reformation in retrospect: *The Victory of Faith over Heresy* (1695–9) by R. Legros, from the altar of St Ignatius in the Gesù, Rome

First American edition 1968

First published as a Norton paperback 1979

ISBN 0-393-95086-7

W.W. Norton & Company, Inc.
500 Fifth Avenue, New York, N.Y. 10110

Printed and bound in Singapore

2 3 4 5 6 7 8 9 0

CONTENTS

Counter Reformation or Catholic Reformation? Was it not quite obviously both? Some of the tributaries to the stream of revival are discernible before Luther. And even after Luther's revolt, the highest Catholic achievements were those of men and women who believed themselves to be seeking Christ rather than fighting Luther. Yet on the other hand, it seems equally clear that the Catholic Reformation was a slow starter and the Lutheran Reformation an exceedingly rapid one. Before the Catholic movement had made significant progress and long before it had captured the Papacy, it found itself confronted by one of the two greatest schisms in the whole history of the Church. Undoubtedly this crisis stimulated self-reforming Catholicism to greater effort, while the tasks of self-defence and counter-attack demanded no small share of its growing resources. In view of these facts, either title remains acceptable, and in this book I shall try to use each in its appropriate place: Catholic Reformation for the more spontaneous manifestations, Counter Reformation for the developed movement with resistance and reconquest high on its agenda. Here I can hardly expect to achieve invariable precision and consistency, but this is no book for pedants.

In addition I hope to make it clear that this Reformation went far beyond these two simple ideas, that it involved not only a sharpening of Catholic definitions but a choice between rival emphases offered to the Catholic Church. To explain these complications with tolerable clarity, I shall first attempt to describe a multilateral context of ideas, religious and otherwise: the long-term effects of late medieval piety and scholasticism, of humanism both secular and biblical, of the various anticlerical and antipapal forces. Above all, one must consider with much care those strong but varying stresses upon St Paul and St Augustine which did not merely help to produce Luther and Calvin, but took very deep root in the thought of many loyal Catholics. The first three chapters will seek to describe the somewhat confused and amorphous world from which the Catholic Reformation gradually liberated itself. Thereafter will follow what is substantially a narrative, or rather a series of intertwined narratives interspersed with some analytical passages. And needless to add, a book four times this length would be far easier to write, if not to read!

When this book was finished but before it went to press, Dr John Bossy very kindly sent me advance proofs of the late H. O. Evennett's Birkbeck Lectures, since published as *The Spirit of the Counter-Reformation*. Despite my admiration for these lectures and for Dr Bossy's brilliant editing and extension of their text, I decided not to make any alterations at this late stage to my own book. The insights of Mr Evennett and his editor are far better studied in their own work than in the form of such condensations as I could have added here. Moreover, the approaches and objectives of the two books are so clearly different that I trust they may be accepted as quite complementary. At least I am bold enough to hope that my broad and earthy survey will in some small degree help readers to appreciate Evennett's more specialized, more intimate and sensitive studies.

My grateful thanks are due to Dr T. M. Parker and to Dr John Bossy, who both read the book in typescript. The former supplied a good many modifications and corrections throughout the book, while the latter revised the paragraphs on Elizabethan Catholicism, greatly to their benefit. I am much indebted to three members of my publisher's staff: Mr Baron, Mrs Kaine and Mrs Bruckner; the last-named discovered the greater part of the illustrations.

I CRITICS AND CONTROLLERS OF THE CHURCH

In 1449 the Papacy brought to an end the Council of Basle and so for the time being triumphed over the dangerous series of attempts to diminish its authority and to reform the Church, perhaps even rule it, through General Councils. Yet by the end of the century the Renaissance popes found themselves plunged into a new crisis of confidence, a crisis arising from a generation more sophisticated and more censorious than any of its predecessors. It was a time when many small men became heirs of the old heresiarchs Marsiglio and Wycliffe, transcended the old disputes over papal authority and began to question the whole status, ministry and organization of the Church. And at the roots of both Protestant and Catholic Reformations there lay in every country of Europe a strong element of protest against ecclesiastical abuses of various kinds.

Forty years ago Lucien Febvre sought to minimize the causal role of such abuses, but it can hardly be said that Europeans were minimizing them on the eve of Martin Luther's revolt. No references to the popes are more brutal and contemptuous than those of Italians like Francesco Guicciardini, who had spent long years in the papal service. Gerhard Ritter has summarized what he calls 'the huge mass of the German nation's grievances against Roman irregularities', which 'had flowed from decade to decade to the steps of the papal throne in a thick, dirty stream.'

From 1510 these *gravamina* were systematically compiled, and eight years later the Augsburg Diet voted to withhold financial aid against the Turk until they should be remedied by the pope. Every Diet resounded with complaints against the bestowal of benefices on monasteries and on papal favourites, against the inordinate and costly prolongation of suits at Rome, against increasing papal taxation, against the undermining of episcopal authority through the sale of exemptions and privileges by the Roman Curia, against scores of other abuses real and imaginary. Ranke discussed the popular literature of the period 1490–1520: Brant's *Ship of Fools* (1494), the *Shrovetide Plays*, the *Eulenspiegel* and the famous version of *Reynard the Fox* published at Lübeck in 1498, and he asked what single characteristic they had in common. His answer was 'hostility to the Church of Rome'.

To the German list we might add a number of slightly later books like the fearless and prophetic sermons of Geiler von Kaisersberg, published by his friends in 1511. Most famous and readable of all were the *Letters of Obscure Men* (1515, 1517), directed by Crotus Rubeanus and Ulrich von Hutten not against the Papacy, but against those suspicious Cologne Dominicans who were persecuting the great Hebraist Reuchlin. The work of Sebastian Brant passed through some twenty-six editions, but in the Latin-reading world its fame was eclipsed by that of Erasmus (c. 1466–1536), whose anti-clerical satire was more urbane in form but no kindlier to the Church, for it struck at cherished principles as well as at abuses and ignorant men. In 1504 his *Enchiridion* impugned the invocation of saints, fasting and indulgences, while in his *Praise of Folly* (1509) and in some of his *Colloquies* (1518) he repeated these attacks to far more devastating effect. *The Praise of Folly* also shows a deep contempt for the scholastic theologians, whose work was to remain basic to

2 The gullible laity as farmyard animals, with kings as lions: woodcut from *Reynard the Fox* (Lübeck 1498)

...ja domi remanferit,
quæ apud Nafonem
transformatorū libro
octauo fic, Tangit &
ira deos,at nō impu/
ne feremus Quæq;
inhonoratæ, nō & di
cemur iultæ, Inquit,
& Oeneos ultorem
fpreta per agros, Mi
fit aprum. De hac re
mult² eft iocus apud
Lucianum, in conui/
uio philofophorū,fi/
ue Lapithis. Tufcu
lum.) Thure olim li/
tabant & mola. Plini
us in præfatione, Et
mola tantum falfa li/
tant,qui non habent
thura. Eft autem mo
la far toftum,fale cō/

Supſtitio / fus cultus imaginum

...minum execratur &
diuus Hieronymus i
epiftolis,qui pugnas
cum dæmōibus,atq;
huiufmodi pertenta
confingunt. Sacrifi
cis & concionatori/
bus.) Palam eft, hic
non reprehendi mira
cula, fed conficta, &
cōficta ad quæftum,
quo plus extorque/
difficillime credūt, q ma
/di fabulamētis,maxime
oritas. Videē aūt taxare
/cant,q circūferentes fan/
ulū huiufmodi portenta
emū Chriftophorum.)
gantea magnitudine fin
tnente ingreffum undag
eidos fic defcribit, Mon
i manu pinus regit,& ue

Supſtitio / fus imagi/ nū cultus.

⸿ Von vnnutzen Buchern
Das ich fitz vornan in dem fchyff
Das hat woilich eyn fundren gryff
On vrfach ift das nit gethan
Auff mein liberey ich mich verlan
Von Buchern haß ich groſſen hort
Verſtand doch drynñ gar wenig wort
Vnd halt fie dannocht in den eren
Das ich in wil der fliegen weren
Wo man von kunften reden thūt

3, 4, 5 Left, saint cults ridiculed in drawings
by Holbein for Erasmus's *Praise of Folly*
(Basel 1515). Above, the pseudo-scholar,
with his useless books and lack of
Christian love, satirized by Brant

Catholicism, but who are here pilloried as intellectual monsters,
claiming to fathom the deeper mysteries of the Trinity and disputing
whether God could have come to redeem man in the form of a
woman, a devil or an ass. Erasmian ridicule did not necessarily spare
Rome itself: the tract *Julius Exclusus* (1517), commonly attributed to
Erasmus, shows St Peter driving the bellicose pope from the gates
of paradise.

11

In assigning Erasmus a place among the anticlericals and the sceptics, one must not forget that other and devouter Erasmus who aspired to see untutored men embrace the personality of Christ, the scholar who abandoned scholasticism only to spend much of his life editing the New Testament and the Fathers. Moreover, his critical attitudes had been more than anticipated by his predecessors, the Italian humanists of the fifteenth century. That the latter seldom openly attacked the Church should not deceive us, for they simply regarded whole sectors of ecclesiastical life as irrelevant to the ends of man. To Ficino and the exalted neo-Platonists of Florence just as to Pomponazzi and the scientific neo-Aristotelians of Padua, the popular religion of miracles, relics, images and indulgences was not worthy even of a contemptuous gesture.

Looking thence at the other Catholic extreme, these humanists likewise disregarded Thomism and the other major scholastic systems, already weakened by Occamist negations and by the haughty aversion of Petrarch. The humanists thought in terms of modest and limited objectives. They rejected a theology which wanted to probe the secrets of the Godhead. They rejected a philosophy which tried to comprehend the whole universe in its neat verbal categories. Long before Luther, Petrarch wrote that the world of God is closed, so far as concerns the finite mind of man, with seven seals. The humanists did not demolish but merely abandoned the cathedral of medieval Christian thought; their sheer lack of wonder at its lofty vaults—as well as their revulsion from its gargoyles—would henceforth set special problems to any Catholic reconstruction. Nevertheless, without intending to do so, they created some tools serviceable for such a project. Their world was that of the grammarian, the philologist, the rhetorician; it contained methods of communication and propaganda superior to those of the Middle Ages. Time was to show that these multi-purpose techniques could be employed as readily by Catholic traditionalists as by critics of the Church.

The French anticlericals of this period can only be understood in the context of their national problems. Against the more onerous Roman encroachments the kingdom of France was ostensibly protected by the Pragmatic Sanction of Bourges (1438), which had asserted the right of the French Church to manage its temporal possessions free of papal intervention, and had debarred papal appointments to French benefices. The kings of France had nevertheless failed to maintain these liberties with any great consistency, and even after 1500 the Pragmatic Sanction remained a centre-point of controversy. In 1513 its text was republished with strongly worded commentaries by the jurist Cosme Guymier, while the Sorbonne theologian Jacques Almain in *The Authority of the Church* (1512) made a powerful attack on the rival papal claims, recently advanced by Cajetan, general of the Dominicans. Of greater interest to the social historian is the group of French vernacular writings partly inspired by these old disputes but much sharpened by the political quarrel of 1511–15 between Louis XII and Julius II. These were rather more than ephemeral tracts; their distaste extends beyond the pope into a general criticism of abuses, and some were still being read long after Louis and Julius had passed from the scene. In his *Treatise on the Difference between Schisms and Councils* (1511), the famous *rhétoriqueur* Jean Lemaire des Belges condemned the Papacy by reference not merely to its present faults but to its whole history.

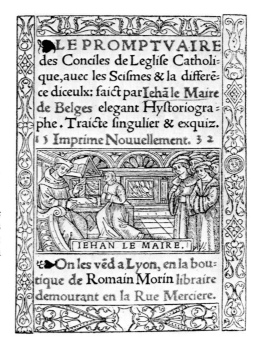

6 Jean Lemaire's *Schisms and Councils* (1511) was frequently republished: title-page of 1532 edition

13

Armed with the Donation of Constantine, happily proved a forgery by Lorenzo Valla, the popes had continually provoked schisms and quarrels throughout Christendom. Gregory VII, continues Lemaire, had ruined ecclesiastical discipline by imposing celibacy on the secular clergy. On the other hand, the kings of Europe, especially those of France, had ever sought to pacify Christendom by means of General Councils. The sultan of Turkey is a better ruler than our present quarrelsome and military pope. We can only hope that the kings will achieve concord despite him, and that the efforts of the French Church will lead to a reforming General Council for the whole of Christendom. While Jean Lemaire had served as secretary and chronicler in the exalted households of Margaret of Austria and Anne of Brittany, this Gallican literature had in general a middle-class and even a popular background; some of it even arose from the Paris theatre of the period. Here the chief author was Pierre Gringore, a leading figure in the play-producing fraternity known as the Companions of the Prince of Fools. With the heavy didacticism and personification beloved by the *rhétoriqueurs* Gringore combined some hard-hitting satire and farce at the expense of the Papacy. In *The Hunt of the Stag* (1510) he describes how the *francs veneurs* (the pun is not over-subtle) will run down the papal 'beast' in his thicket. In *The Prince of Fools* (1512) he introduces the personified vices Simony and Hypocrisy, who are at last converted by the menaces of Divine Punishment; but one figure remains unredeemed to the end: the Obstinate Man (Julius II) who admits to lies, injustices, love of money, high living and drunkenness. On the other hand, Gringore was no heretic or mocking agnostic; some of his writings suggest a warm piety and in later years he was to denounce the Lutheran heresy in the strongest terms.

A third *rhétoriqueur*, Jean Bouchet, joined Gringore in attacking not merely papal misdeeds but clerical avarice and debauchery in general; both also condemned the hypocrisy of so-called reforming prelates and canons, who should begin by reforming themselves. Bouchet, an attorney from Poitiers and later a friend of Rabelais, was an imitator of Brant's *Ship of Fools*, which had been translated into French as early as 1500. Like Brant and Erasmus, he satirized not merely the clergy but all mankind, yet he reserved a special venom for the 'mitred asses', the soft-living priests and the undisciplined monks. His *Lamentation of the Church Militant* (1512) does not directly support the royal policies, but bewails the ruin of the Church by avarice, simony and pluralism. Despite the sins of a pope who makes war on Christian states, Bouchet counsels the king to participate in the Lateran Council called by Julius, as well as to discipline the French clergy and turn the power of Christendom against the Turk.

During these years the critical spirit in England was not exacerbated by anglo-papal quarrels, yet its presence may be felt in many places. The Wycliffite or Lollard heresy had survived and was nothing if not anticlerical. Yet during the years following 1500 it remained an underground movement divorced from the ruling class and without access to the printing presses. As so often in history, the most vocal critics of the clergy arose from among themselves and proposed conservative reform. The *Exhortatory Sermon* (1510) by Chancellor Melton of York and the equally outspoken sermons preached by his friend Dean Colet to the Provincial Council of 1510 and the Convocation of 1512 all systematically detail the covetousness, ignorance, loose living and worldly preoccupations of the English clergy in terms which can only have applied to a minority. A layman's deduction appears in *The Tree of Commonwealth*, written in 1509–10 by the lawyer Edmund Dudley, one of Henry VII's enterprising ministers known to taxpayers as 'ravening wolves'. Dudley here claims that the king is not merely the protector but the overseer of the English Church; he appoints the bishops and is responsible for making them establish discipline. He must, moreover, adjudge all disputes between clergy and laity. 'And no man', Dudley concludes, 'can do it but the Prince.'

In 1514–15 there occurred a mass demonstration of anticlericalism by the citizens of London, provoked by the murder of the suspected heretic Richard Hunne in the bishop's prison at St Paul's. These riots were followed by attacks in Parliament upon benefit of clergy and by a quarrel between the lay judges and the bishops in the presence of the young Henry VIII. During subsequent years the literary assault upon the clergy, and especially upon the unpopular Cardinal Wolsey, came in large part from the common lawyers, most of whom were interested in abasing the ecclesiastical courts rather than in reforming the Church. Their distinguished leader Christopher St German sought nothing less than the exaltation of state over church, and he survived to become in his old age a literary champion of the Henrician schism. Meanwhile this hostility towards the Church was merging with the incoming stream of Lutheranism, which during the 1520s invaded the universities, the merchant class of the ports, even the rural Lollard communities. The most blistering English attack upon clerical vices, *A Supplication for the Beggars* (1529), came from the lawyer Simon Fish, a prominent figure among these early Protestants. He also translated into his own language the somewhat radical Protestant handbook *The Sum of Scripture*, which was to attain seven editions in England between 1529 and 1550. Yet the English literature of protest is anticlerical rather than antipapal: little English money was now going to Rome, while the legate Wolsey attracted malevolence which might otherwise have been directed against his papal masters or against ecclesiastical abuses in general. Until his overthrow these attacks had to be surreptitious, but they were numerous and headed by John Skelton, the ablest English poet and satirist of the day. When in 1529 Wolsey fell and the Reformation Parliament began to curtail the jurisdiction and privileges of the Church, the stage had been well set for profounder revolutions. Within four years the king, unable to gain his divorce from Habsburg-dominated Rome, had little difficulty in leading his subjects into a national schism.

Throughout the Middle Ages there had been the closest links between the anticlericalism of subjects and the erastianism of rulers. Ministers and jurists throughout the transalpine lands had lost few opportunities to refuse the demands and dispute the claims of the popes. In the fourteenth century, Dubois, Marsiglio, Occam, Wycliffe and other thinkers, mostly servants of temporal rulers and magnates, had sought to tear the theory of papal monarchy to shreds. Likewise, when Henry VIII quarrelled with Clement VII he had at his disposal a number of old statutes still useful to daunt his own clergy and to exclude papal jurisdiction from his realm. When

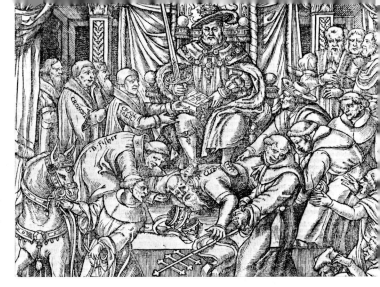

7 Henry VIII, accompanied by Cranmer, triumphs over Clement VII and Cardinal John Fisher: woodcut from Foxe, 1569 edition

in 1516 Francis I and Leo X temporarily patched up the franco-papal feud, the former did more than recover the safeguards of the Pragmatic Sanction. By the Concordat of Bologna he received from the pope a hitherto unknown measure of control over the French Church, in which he was now empowered to nominate the holders of some 620 leading offices in cathedrals and monasteries. During the remainder of this century and throughout the next, the new Gallicanism under royal leadership often seemed an opponent of the Papacy only less formidable than Protestantism itself. Yet it remained a political not a spiritual force. The French Church could not debate on equal terms with the Church of Rome because the French state prevented it from speaking with a united voice. The French spirit never came to dominate the Catholic Reformation, at least until its late phases in the seventeenth century. In religion as in politics, Valois France, potentially the greatest power of Europe, was locked in domestic tensions and signally failed to dominate the age.

Nowhere did there exist a more vigorous erastianism than that of the Crowns of Castile and Aragon under Ferdinand and Isabella. These rulers ensured that only prelates devoted to their interests should be presented to the Spanish sees; they annexed the masterships and the revenues of the great military Orders; they used the Inquisition for political ends. Long after the end of their campaigns

17

against the Moors, they extorted from the pope most of the proceeds from great campaigns of indulgence-selling which purported to be funding further crusades. For them the Spanish Pope Alexander VI divided the New World between Spain and Portugal, giving the lion's share to the former. But even Alexander refused when they demanded the appointment of a transatlantic patriarch who should be in effect a Latin-American pope under their management. Most sinister of all their controls was the one imposed by their conquest of the kingdom of Naples (1495–1504). This success gave them a local grip upon Rome subsequently exploited to great effect by their Habsburg successors. Here was a disconcerting situation for less advantageously placed rulers and nations, an obvious peril for Roman pontiffs who wanted to preserve some freedom of action or some semblance of impartiality between Christian nations near and far.

From this time forward the kings of Spain seldom bestowed their services upon the Papacy and the Church Universal save at a heavy price. To define that price must be an objective of any historian of the Counter Reformation, for that movement developed alongside, and in conjunction with, the rise of Spain to a position of near-hegemony in Europe. Viewed superficially, the Habsburgs appear to stand high among the preservers of Catholicism. Yet does not closer inspection reveal their dangerous interference with all the nations from England to Hungary, the boundless dynastic ambitions which caused them to exploit the Papacy and so alienate the nations from a papalism too often manipulated in their Habsburg family interests? Heaven should have preserved Rome from her friends as much as from her foes. Rather than inhabit a Christendom under Habsburg chairmanship, a host of determined Dutchmen, Englishmen, Germans and even Frenchmen found themselves prepared—at whatever religious cost—to make do with mere national churches. By 1529 Spanish rule was also firmly established in Milan and the whole Italian peninsula was expiating the follies of its once-vaunted Renaissance rulers. As for the popes, they retained some influence both as Italian princes and still more as leaders of Catholic Christendom, yet there were times when they could do little more than writhe angrily in the talons of the Habsburg eagle.

The period of decline in medieval Catholicism nourished many of the seedlings of Catholic Reformation. Among the features of the latter stands a notable revival of scholastic philosophy and especially of Thomism. Yet this revival had in fact begun among the Dominicans over half a century before the birth of its greatest figure Francisco de Suarez (1548–1617). Thomas de Vio, later famous as Cardinal Cajetan (1469–1534), composed his treatise on the *De Ente et Essentia* of Aquinas while teaching at Padua in 1494–7. His famous commentaries on the *Summa Theologica* followed between 1507 and 1522: the first great monument of this neo-Thomism, they remain among the classics of the revival. Between 1520 and the rise of Thomist theory throughout the Council of Trent, the movement was defended by Domingo Soto and others against the attacks of biblical humanism. As the Dominicans had resuscitated Thomism, so in the fifteenth century the Franciscans had fostered Scotism, a less powerful and integrated tradition, yet one which was to inspire a succession of philosophers into and even beyond the seventeenth century. Today its points of divergence from Thomism may well seem to non-specialists quite marginal, yet they served to give life to the scholasticism of the sixteenth century and to prevent it from becoming monolithic. Alongside these revivals stood the classical or humanist tradition, literary, philological, historical and antiquarian, which so powerfully influenced many aspects of Catholic reform from the decrees of the Council of Trent to the education provided by the Jesuits. Like the Protestant Reformation, that of Catholicism made a distinctly selective approach to the work of the humanists, yet the latter did much to shape it, and they represented a tradition already—at least in Italy—some two and a half centuries old by the time of Trent.

Such were among the main intellectual foundations of the new Catholic world, and its spirituality was equally deep-rooted in tradition. Devotional books and concepts emanating from the fourteenth century were still lively in some circles during much of the seventeenth. Even the great figures in whom we find more originality and personal inspiration were nevertheless dependent at some phases of their development upon medieval instruments of devotion. At innumerable points, the new growth was firmly grafted upon the old. While recovering in 1521 from his painful wound at his father's castle of Loyola, the young Ignatius had exhausted the romances of chivalry when his thoughts were led into more serious channels by chance encounters with *The Flower of Saints*, a Spanish adaptation of *The Golden Legend*, and with the famous *Life of Christ* by the fourteenth-century Carthusian Ludolph of Saxony. These and similar books later left their marks upon Loyola's *Spiritual Exercises*. A more debatable inspiration came from the *Exercises of the Spiritual Life*, composed for monks as recently as 1500 by García de Cisneros, the Benedictine abbot of Montserrat. Yet undoubtedly the chief medieval influence upon Loyola's spiritual

8, 9, 10 Popular piety.
Left to right, woodcut
from Spanish edition of
The Flower of Saints
(*c.* 1500); angels rescuing
souls in a French version
of *The Golden Legend*
(1483); a bonfire of
vanities from J. Stumpf,
Swiss Chronicle (1548)

11 St Bernardino of Siena
(d. 1444), the great
Franciscan revivalist
of fifteenth-century Italy:
dotted print, *c.* 1454

life was the *Imitation of Christ* (*c.* 1418), the great monument of the 'new piety', the *devotio moderna* of the Netherlands. This famous book Ignatius first read at Manresa: in his own words, he 'preferred it ever afterwards to any other book of devotion.' The *Exercises* of St Ignatius are of course predominantly meditative rather than mystical; they lead the mind through an ordered sequence of holy themes and images; they do not seek to empty the mind of images in order to make way for the indescribable 'states' of the mystic. Yet the two methods are not mutually exclusive; they had fused together in the *devotio moderna*, and, as we shall shortly argue, Ignatius and some other Jesuits were to retain more of the old mystical tradition than is commonly supposed.

Among the greatest names in Jesuit history is that of the Dutchman Peter Canisius, who soon after joining the Society published (1543) *The True Evangelical Life: Divine Sermons, Teachings, Letters, Songs and Prophecies.* These are taken partly from the works of Johann Tauler, the fourteenth-century mystic who had so deeply influenced Luther, but they also incorporate a number of other old Rhenish and Netherlandish writings, including important extracts from Ruysbroeck. Again, as St Teresa of Avila strove to discipline her spiritual impulses, she learned much from the recent Spanish mystics, Laredo, Osuna and her personal counsellor St Peter of Alcántara; yet she was also very familiar with the *Imitation of Christ* and with St Augustine's *Confessions*, while in her autobiography she also cites St Vincent Ferrer (d. 1419) and Ludolph of Saxony. A Spaniard among Spaniards, she nevertheless derived far more than she can have realized from Netherlanders of former generations, since in the *Third Alphabet* of Francisco de Osuna she was in fact imbibing mystical ideas derived from Thomas à Kempis, Ruysbroeck and Jan Mombaer. Still more striking are the continuities observable in the religious life of Italy. The Oratory which grew around St Philip Neri in Rome during the 1550s and 1560s lies at the very heart of the Catholic Reformation, and we know in detail what books were used as starting-points by his famous discussion groups. The list, highly traditional in character, forms a select bibliography of medieval devotional authors: Richard of St Victor,

SEQVERE·ME

12, 13, 14, 15 Four editions of the ubiquitous *Imitation of Christ*, then attributed to Gerson:
English (London 1504); Latin (Venice 1524); Spanish (Alcalá 1555); Latin (Cologne 1501)

**Libro de la Imita-
ció de Chriſto: llamado Cótemp-
tus Mundi. Nueuamente romança
do có ſu tabla. Viſto y corregido a-
gora de nueuo impreſſo en Al
cala: en el Año de
1 5 5 5.**

Liber de imitatõe Chriſti
Cum tractatu de medita
tione Cordis.

Innocent III, Denis the Carthusian, St Catherine of Siena, various Franciscan writers and the hymns of Jacopone da Todi (d. 1306), reputed author of the *Stabat Mater*.

In the Netherlands the continuity of the *devotio moderna* is especially impressive. During the later sixteenth century few devotional writers became more popular in the Catholic areas than François–Louis de Blois (Blosius, 1506–66) the Benedictine abbot of Liessies in Hainault. A reformer in his Order, he wrote with exceptional clarity 'for simple but earnest people', and his *Institutio Spiritualis* (1551) has long been accepted as a classic of its school. But despite its date the book belongs wholly to the *devotio moderna*. The favourite author of Abbot Blosius is Johann Tauler, and he is closely followed by Suso, Ruysbroeck, the Victorines and a number of twelfth- and thirteenth-century mystics. In this old tradition Blosius gently conducts his readers up the ladder of mystical prayer. Though he accepts the meditative technique ('picture-making') as helpful in the earlier phases, he looks forward to the stage when the devout man or woman will be able to abandon these crutches. Meanwhile, in France, the translation and printing of the late medieval mystics began with Lefèvre of Étaples (*c.* 1455–1536), the famous biblical humanist and student of mysticism who stands so ambivalently between Catholic and Protestant reform. Between 1570 and 1620 there followed very numerous editions both in French and Latin. They included not only modern contemplatives like St Teresa and Luis de Granada, but also Denis the Carthusian, Suso, Tauler, Catherine of Genoa, Angela of Foligno and others of the earlier age. From this stage, as Frenchmen made their most weighty contributions to the revival of Catholic spirituality, their debt direct and indirect to medieval tradition remains clear enough.

Similar things may also be said of the persecuted Catholics in Elizabethan and early Stuart England; still more of the many English Catholics then exiled on the Continent. The martyr of York, Margaret Clitherow (d. 1586), was a convert from Anglicanism and by that fact a significant figure of the Counter Reformation. During the 1570s her main reading was in the *Imitation of Christ* and in the recent *Spiritual Exercises* (1557) of the Dominican William Peryn, who derived both from Loyola and from medieval sources. The *Imitation* is again prominent among the books of Catholics who built up a community life in their prisons, like Father William Davies and his companions of the early 1590s in Beaumaris Castle. By this time the chief surviving master in the mystical tradition was an English exile; the Capuchin Benedict Canfield (d. 1611). Through him this tradition descended to numerous continental disciples including his fellow Capuchin Père Joseph, the *éminence grise* of Richelieu. Amongst the English their own native mystical heritage had also survived. During the reign of Mary Tudor pious Catholics like Richard Whitford and Robert Parkyn were writing devotional essays with close affinities to Richard Rolle and to that greater contemplative Walter Hilton. Even in the seventeenth century Father Augustine Baker (d. 1641) was introducing his English nuns at Cambrai to these old mystics, and observing that by this time a Latin translation might help them with the antiquated English. Even after the Restoration of 1660 these same writings were still being studied by Serenus Cressy in the household of Queen Catherine of Braganza.

Since Spanish mysticism stands among the most striking phenomena of the Catholic Reformation, the problems surrounding its origin assume a special importance at this stage of our inquiry. The interest of Spaniards in this approach to religion was not limited to a handful of choice spirits: it became almost a literary mass-movement. Menendez y Pelayo calculated the number of mystical works in print or in manuscript as amounting to some three thousand. Mystical authors can be numbered in hundreds between 1500 and 1675, around which latter date the school went into steep decline with the Quietist Miguel de Molinos. Many of these writers, it is true, were analysts of mysticism, or even sentimental romantics, rather than first-hand practitioners. 'No one', writes Allison Peers, 'can appreciate the depths to which they can descend who has not read some of the worst.' Interest has nevertheless tended to centre unduly upon the towering figures of St Teresa and St John of the Cross, before whom at least half a dozen major contemplative writers, mostly Franciscans, were active. The two great Carmelites should indeed be seen not in isolation but as the highest peaks in an impressive mountain range which also included such figures as Luis de Granada (d. 1585), St Peter of Alcántara (d. 1562) and Luis de Leon (d. 1591).

This school emerges with dramatic suddenness in the year 1500 with the works of Gómez García and García de Cisneros, all the more dramatically since during the previous two centuries, the contribution of Spaniards to mystical literature had proved almost negligible. For the sudden flaring of this experience and literature no single factor can account. Several specialist scholars and historians of literature have frankly ascribed it—especially in the case of Cisneros —to belated Netherlandish and German influences from the worlds of Tauler and the *devotio moderna*. Even where overt links do not appear, the close similarities of theme and method cannot be wholly due to coincidence. Again, some of the Spanish mystics show obvious debts to the neo-Platonism of Ficino, Pico and other Italians of the High Renaissance. On the other hand, it seems equally clear that about 1500 the Spanish mind stood prepared not merely to accept these foreign influences but to develop them further than they had hitherto been developed in the West. In examining the writings of the great Carmelites one finds more inducement to stress their independence than their traditionalism. Neverthe-less, the Castilian temperament with its strange blend of morosity and ardour is a factor which no one who knows this people will ever take lightly. Even in the Spain of our own day it is impossible to avoid being struck by a capacity for ecstatic worship, an idealism which counts the world well lost for a cause. Medieval Spain had infused these qualities of mind into the harsh tasks of warfare against the infidel, and after the conquest of Moorish Granada they flowed into new channels: into the interior life, into military adventure and imperialism. There seems to have occurred a cultural release com-parable with that which occurred in the northern Netherlands a century later, when the Dutch first savoured their newly-born independence and nationhood. Yet again, the Spanish Church was the first to experience rigorous reform; and while the accidents of individual genius must not be discounted, the growing host of monks,

ri'nisi p assiduã suoꝛ beneficioꝛ ꝓsideratiõem. nã isti sunt
funiculitqbus trabimur aptamur τ adberemus deo f; ꝗõ
ipse p ꝓpbetã Osee testaf oscẽs. Trabam eos in funiculis
Adam. Et ꝗ ft; fratres funiculi Adã nisi omutuoꝛ munemu;
sugis ruminatio vt Liconiẽs τ Bonauẽtura oiciũt: Angel
ter sicut nobis insudandũ est vt in bmissio exercitio assidue
nosipos crescendi pietam babeam°. τ ꝓculdubio expiemur
aias ñras diuiniti° illuminari τ inflãmari. qꝛ vt brũs Aug°.
dicit: nibil nos ita ad dei inflãmat amoꝛe sicut crebra dis
uinoꝛũ beneficioꝛ recoꝛdatio.

Capl'm sertium

Queadmodũ supra di rim° nõ
solum ꝓnobis ipsis sed ꝓ toto mũdo
orare τ totis pietatis visceribus sup
plicare debemus oĩm. quaten° suam
dignetur inclinare misccõiam ad oẽs
creaturas: ꝓ quibus princeps glorie
christus redẽptoꝛ noster pati dignat?
est: vt.f. ad agnitiõe; ꝟitat? siue catholice fidei trabatur si=
ue rꝑsant siue iudei siue alt infideles ꝟnõ priuent illo brõ=
rũ ꝓsortio felicissimo τ careãt illa btifica diuinitat? visiõe:
ad cui° ꝓtẽplatiõe; τ fruitiõe; rõnales creature fuerũt ꝓdi=
te. Pro qb° quoꝗ τ sanguis rpi ꝑciosus thesaur? fu it effu
sus i cruce. Precipue tñ diuinã artamur ꝓ ppło rpiano sup
plicare maiestatẽ sic nos docet Dieremias ꝓpbã: cũ videõ
ppłs suũ p liquũ rege nabuchodonosoꝛ male tractari τ cap
tiuũ i babylonẽ trabi dolẽs aiebat.ꝗo dabit capiti mo aquã
τ oclis meis fõte lacriaꝝ:τ plorabo die ac nocte iterfectos

16 Contents and chapter-heading from García de Cisneros, *Exercises of the Spiritual Life* (1500)

friars and nuns provided seed-beds incomparably larger than those
of any other European nation.

Despite the remarkable phenomena of Protestant 'spiritualist'
religion, it must be acknowledged that the Western mystical tradition has in general been closely linked with monasticism, which
alone afforded conditions making for the higher degrees of mental
concentration. And if one Order be singled out as a special nurse of
this tradition, it should certainly be that of the Carthusians, whose
external influence—considering the enclosed character of their rule—
proved surprisingly widespread and extended to many members of
other Orders. Even so, it would seem unrealistic to 'explain' the
Catholic revival chiefly by reference to spiritual enterprise on these
exalted levels. The Netherlandish *devotio moderna* and its parallels
elsewhere in Europe owed much to the high mystics, yet it nurtured
in its offspring a mild and beneficent pietism, a spiritual integrity
rather than a sense of close union with the divine. These people were

27

mostly literate, middle-class laymen and laywomen, or else secular priests also living the 'active' life. As they read the *Imitation of Christ* and the numerous guides written in its spirit, they did not very seriously aspire to scale the pinnacles of religious experience. But alongside the immense output of hagiographical and other books catering for the mere popular cults, there grew throughout the early and middle decades of the sixteenth century an extensive literature dealing with the interior life and largely intended for the use of people in the world as distinct from the cloister. These range from simple primers to sophisticated guides, mostly in fact by members of religious Orders. They include the works by Cisneros and his Spanish successors, those of Giovanni Battista Carioni (d. 1534) and Serafino Aceto da Pratis (d. 1534) in Italy, of William Bonde (*fl.* 1500–30), Richard Whitford (d. *c.* 1555) and William Peryn (d. 1558) in England, together with a long succession of Netherlanders in the Ruysbroeck tradition from Henry Herp (d. 1477) to Francis Vervoort (d. 1555) and Nicholas van Esch (d. 1578). Little is known about some of these authors. The long-popular *Gospel Pearl* went through a dozen Netherlandish editions and several foreign translations; it was ascribed by van Esch merely to a 'holy woman' who died in 1540 at the age of seventy-seven.

Unquestionably this voluminous literature did much to fortify Catholicism in the minds of the middle ranks of European society, and to prepare the way for religious education as methodized by the Jesuits and other teaching Orders. Amongst its authors there figure numerous friars, and no account of the earlier phases of Catholic revival would be complete without a distinct emphasis upon the living spirit of St Francis. Needless to add, this is especially true of the Italian revival. We tend perhaps too often to imagine the Catholic Reformation against a backcloth of harsh sierra and tableland in Castile. At least equally may an imaginative traveller sense its lingering spirit along the shores of Maggiore and Garda; better still in the Franciscan homeland itself, as he gazes from the crest of Assisi across the gentle, velvet distances of Umbria.

III AUGUSTINE AND LUTHER

The Protestant landslide which followed Luther's revolt of 1517–20 engulfed most of Germany and Scandinavia within a couple of decades, and it long seemed certain to engulf Austria. Thereupon Calvin systematized Protestant theology, bound together the greater part of the Swiss in one Reformed religion, began to win a strong foothold in Poland, Hungary, the Netherlands and Scotland. More important still, in the 1550s he sent a powerful force of missionaries into his native France. Save for the brief five years of the Marian Reaction, England remained in schism. She received multiple Protestant influences and ended by developing a national Church which, though neither Lutheran nor Calvinist, was quite distinctly Protestant in character. These events seemed to presage further victories, possibly something approaching a complete triumph for the new Churches. Luther himself never thought he was imposing permanent divisions upon Christendom: he firmly believed that the Papacy lay under God's curse and was hence literally moribund. From the 1530s to the 1550s, even cautious observers thought Catholicism would be fortunate to retain the allegiance of Italy and the Iberian peninsula. Why had this landslide happened? And why was it ultimately arrested? The causes are both complex and debatable; their respective weights must remain uncertain, yet they must in some measure be defined before one may begin to assess the context, the boundaries or the full achievement of the Counter Reformation. We have already indicated one major factor: the growing bitterness of an anticlericalism long endemic in medieval society. Yet alongside this negative factor, Protestantism developed its own positive dynamic, one which made Luther's expectations of total victory at least intelligible.

In some regions, it is true, earlier heretical movements had prepared the way. The Hussites in Bohemia-Moravia, the Waldensians in the south-western Alpine valleys and in scattered Italian groups, the Lollards in various parts of England all survived and entered into significant alliances with the new Protestantism. Yet none of these supplied Luther, Zwingli, Bucer or Calvin with their theological and social concepts, and by this time none retained much capacity for independent expansion. Hussitism, the one which had been midwife to the birth of a nation, had also supplied Europe with a sad cautionary tale, arising from its own internal divisions and civil wars. In any event, there were limitations to the ability of Slavs to influence Germans or western Europeans. Meanwhile, both the Waldensians and the Lollards stood in the position of hard-pressed partisans: desperately short of modern weapons, they awaited liberation at the hands of the well-equipped Protestant invaders.

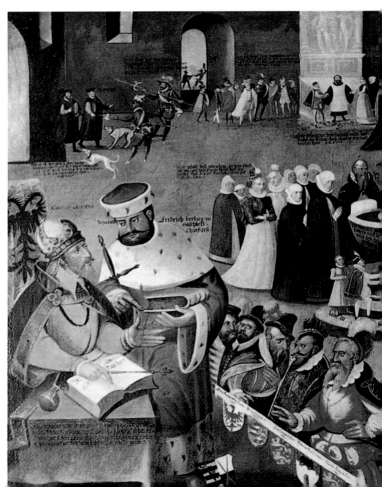

17 A tableau of Protestant religion (1601) in the Town Hall, Windsheim: marriage, baptism, communion, preaching, singing, etc. At left, Charles V finds fault with the Confession of Augsburg while John Frederick of Saxony produces the *Apologia*. Bottom centre, Protestant princes and officials of Imperial cities

To secular factors the Protestant explosion undoubtedly owed a great deal. But among these, the role of ambitious German and Scandinavian rulers has sometimes been exaggerated. The initial impacts of Protestantism look especially striking within the free cities of the Empire and Switzerland, places where kings and princes exercised little or no influence. Throughout Europe the independent-minded and more or less literate townsman formed the hard brick from which Protestantism could build its churches. The image of the greedy autocrat is not wholly imaginary, yet it may too easily be invoked to explain Lutheran expansion. For the most part the early Lutheran princes were sincere converts who ran immense risks for the religious cause, and in the years 1547–55 they narrowly avoided utter catastrophe. By contemporary standards not a few of them

and their descendants can be labelled 'good rulers', and several used a fair proportion of the secularized Church lands for charitable and educational purposes. Greater material beneficiaries were the nobles and squires who bought these lands, made fortunes from the rise in agricultural profits and successfully strove in the various Estates to control the incomes and powers of their princes.

To an extent no one can have foreseen, the Habsburgs, opponents-in-chief of the Reformation, found their resources so strained by their fight against the French and the Ottoman Turks that they could win no decisive or permanent military advantages over the Lutherans. Below this level of high politics a host of forces affected the outcome of the struggle in the various countries of Europe. In Poland avaricious ecclesiastical landlords and oppressive Church courts helped to turn sections of the gentry towards Lutheranism. Then, since their education was Latin and not German, the gentry turned much more decisively towards Calvinism. In poor, divided Hungary the Turkish occupation had from 1526 destroyed the wealth and freedom of the Catholic Church, and had left much of the country open to Protestant missionaries. In Germany Catholicism became identified with Roman financial exactions, in England with King Philip and Habsburg hegemony, in Scotland with the dynastic ambitions of the Guises. In all these three cases the Church hence clashed with rising national sentiment, and it was not long before the same happened in the Netherlands. For a time the Reformers gained some almost fortuitous allies. The German humanists appear at first to have supported Luther's struggle as a sequel to that between Reuchlin and the Dominicans, between enlightenment and obscurantism. Until Luther openly clashed with Erasmus in 1525, the bleak antithesis between Lutheran Paulinism and Christian humanism was not generally sensed. As yet the laymen who believed the anticlerical publicists tended to think Luther and Erasmus were fighting the same battle side by side. Meanwhile, the peasantries of Europe, even those of Germany, entered the confessional struggle from a more oblique angle. In many areas they proved impervious to the new religious ideas, even resentful of change and addicted to the traditional forms of popular Catholicism. In central, western and southern Germany the peasants misinterpreted Luther's initial call for spiritual freedom as a plea for their delivery from economic and social subjection: in 1524–5 they were disillusioned—though how widely is disputable—when with hysterical violence Luther condemned their revolts.

However deeply Luther disappointed the expectations of the lowest social orders, he involuntarily did much to release fundamentalist, millenarian and spiritualist impulses which neither he nor any 'moderate' Reformers could control. There followed the rise of Anabaptism and of other radical sects, which had already taken root in Luther's shadow in Saxony and in that of Zwingli around Zürich. During the late 1520s and early 1530s this sectarianism spread like wildfire in the small towns and villages of central Europe, even within the relatively tolerant city of Strassburg. It exploited economic depression in the Dutch ports; it found a congenial setting among the shifting communities of miners in the Tyrol and it merged with the left wing of Hussitism in Moravia. Only a minority of the sectarians sought to establish the New Jerusalem by the sword. Nevertheless, the whole movement terrified both the 'moderate' Reformers and the propertied classes, and this especially after the horrific episode of 1534–5 at Münster, where fanatical Anabaptists seized control, sustained a long siege and sought to remodel society along biblical and prophetic lines. At this point we at last encounter an important if negative source of conservative reaction. In the minds of hitherto uncommitted people, such radical excesses combined with the notorious differences of view between 'moderate' Protestants to discredit Protestantism as a whole. The general fear of social and religious chaos helped Catholicism far more than it helped Luther and Calvin. A century and a half before Bossuet wrote his *History of the Variances of the Protestant Churches* (1688), Catholic preachers could go to work effectively upon this theme.

Apart from all these developments, many other agencies affected the spread of new ideas. The steady rise of lay education, the growth of interest in emancipated humanist literature reinforced the spirit of criticism. Between 1450 and 1500 a spate of university-founding helped both to enlarge and to intensify the intellectual ferment.

Though some universities including that of Paris resisted heresy, many others ranged themselves behind Luther and his associates: all with their controversies and sermons provided excellent sounding-boards. More important still was the proliferation of printing presses, which gave the Reformers a weapon hitherto unknown in Christian schisms, and one raised to a new potency by the literary genius of Luther. In nearly every major centre north of the Alps the publishers warmly favoured Protestantism, with the result that throughout the crucial 1520s the output of Protestant books enormously outnumbered that of works by the Catholic defence. By the time Catholic publicists recaptured an adequate sector of the press their cause had sustained some incurable wounds.

35

18, 19, 20 St Augustine in a fifteenth-century French woodcut. Top of page: Lutheran woodcut (1545) of Pope Alexander VI; the lifted flap reveals a monstrous caricature

When every allowance has been made for all these factors, it should probably be acknowledged that the most formidable threat presented to the Catholic Church lay in certain of the actual religious teachings of Protestantism. Luther had not limited his appeal to the attack on particular abuses, but had continued to present all abuses as the inevitable outcome of fundamentally false doctrines. Moreover, he had contended that these errors sprang directly and chiefly from the Papacy itself; in particular from its usurpation of powers over man's salvation which rightfully lay within God's prerogative and could not be delegated to a clerical hierarchy. That critics of abuses should seek some doctrinal reconstructions was in itself no matter for surprise. The growing stress laid by medieval Christianity upon building and the arts, upon liturgical refinements, external observances, the multiplication of endowed requiem Masses, above all upon the cult of saints, relics, shrines and pilgrimages, had already led to spiritual movements which laid a corrective stress upon the interior religion. Tortured by his own sense of inadequacy before the terrifying majesty of God, Luther himself had found comfort in some of these mystical writers, who were also helping to inspire Catholic revival. This corrective he discovered especially in the sermons of Tauler and the *Theologia Germanica*, of which latter he edited printed editions in 1516 and 1518. In addition, Luther's emphasis upon the omnipotence, the 'otherness', the unfathomable depth of the Godhead, owed much to the Occamist tradition in which he had been raised at the university of Erfurt, and which was certainly not considered heretical in the sixteenth century. Nevertheless, if we seek the ancestry of Protestant doctrine we shall find it far less in the mystics or in Occamism than in the study of St Augustine. This study naturally occurred within Luther's own Augustinian Order, but it had long flourished among those Catholic reformers who sought antidotes against human pride and self-sufficiency, or who desired to protest against the commercialization of religion, against anthropocentric versions of God, against over-emphasis upon man's good works as titles to salvation.

By way of contrast most Reformers could find in Augustine all they needed in terms of pessimism about weak, fallen man. Augustine had left little unsaid when it came to stressing human impotence without divine grace, man's justification by faith as opposed to works, and Christ's sacrifice in its all-sufficiency, or God's true omnipotence, when by His inscrutable design He selects one sinner for salvation, another for reprobation. The later Middle Ages show a striking sequence of Augustinian reformers: Archbishop Bradwardine, Gregory of Rimini, Wycliffe, John of Wesel and Wessel Gansfort. Yet Luther was far less a disciple of these writers than a direct student of Augustine's works: he is also known to have been heavily engaged with these emphases as he lectured on Peter Lombard and studied Hugh of St Victor. More relevantly for students of the Catholic Reformation, Luther was also exposed within the tradition of his own Order to a vigorous oral and literary tradition which both preceded and followed him. This tradition can fairly be envisaged as a frontier just within the Catholic empire yet in contiguity with that of Protestantism.

The writings of the fifteenth-century General of Luther's Order, Agostino Favaroni, show lines of thought deriving from Augustine but having a curiously familiar ring for any modern student of Luther. The chief sixteenth-century representative of the tradition was Girolamo Seripando, whom Luther probably met, since as a youth he was already in the convent by the Porta del Popolo where Luther stayed during his famous visit to Rome in 1510–11. Over thirty years later Seripando was being attacked as crypto-Lutheran, whereas he had merely drunk along with the young Luther at the fountainhead of St Augustine. The charge did not stick; later on Seripando became a cardinal and a legate at the Council of Trent.

There did exist in Italy during the 1530s and 1540s a movement claimed by some modern historians as 'Catholic Evangelism'. Yet recently McNair has stressed the considerable degree in which it depended not merely upon Augustine but upon the justificatory teachings of Luther, Zwingli and Calvin. All the known Italian Evangelical cities had been previously subjected to a heavy deluge of Protestant propaganda, the effects of which can be traced in the writings of such groups. Their real leader was Juan de Valdés (d. 1541) whose famous circle in Naples contained Giulia Gonzaga,

Vittoria Colonna and other celebrities. Had he lived slightly longer, Valdés would almost certainly have been involved in heresy proceedings. Within two years of his death, his friends Ochino and Peter Martyr had openly defected to Protestantism, while a third disciple had published in Venice the notorious pamphlet *The Benefit of Christ Crucified* (1543), which taught justification in Lutheran terms, and from 1550 occupied a place in the Index of Prohibited Books. During the brief interval the *Beneficio* had sold forty thousand copies in Venice alone. More strangely, it had been championed for a time by Morone, Pole and at least three other cardinals. Whatever their relationship with Lutheran books, only a limited number of the Italian Evangelicals decided to leave the Church, but their movement was not purely aristocratic or wholly transient. In Venice from 1540 solid citizens commonly made wills expressing in passionate terms their entire dependence on the merits of Christ; this conviction continued for several decades, yet was often combined with the veneration of saints and other Catholic elements.

Hence for some years before and after 1540, the frontier between Augustine and Luther had become heavily blurred. Then the Council of Trent did not merely reject Lutheran doctrines; it also thrust aside the pleas of men like Seripando, who wanted to maintain the older and less radical stress on justification by faith based upon St Augustine. Nevertheless, the Augustinian emphasis soon reasserted itself with the Louvain theologian Michel Baius (d. 1589), whose direct spiritual heirs were the Jansenists. An important stretch of the frontier between Catholicism and Protestantism thus passed through the rugged frontier-province of justification by faith. In theological terms, where exactly was the frontier drawn by Trent and by those who have since upheld the Tridentine decisions? In other words, how far did Luther and Calvin go beyond Augustine as interpreted by Catholic theologians?

For Luther as for others, Augustine's writings led to a direct reexamination of the Pauline Epistles, especially of *Romans*, in which earliest masterpiece of Christian theology may be found Luther's points of departure. Probably about the autumn of 1518 Luther came

21 Man as inspired mouthpiece of the word of God. St Paul with St Mark, from Dürer's *Four Apostles* (1526), one of the very few great sixteenth-century paintings inspired by Protestantism

to the conclusion that Paul meant by justification something different from Augustine's concept. For Augustine as for Paul, man is indeed justified—put into a saving relationship with God—by divine grace and through faith. But Augustine had envisaged this act as a gradual process of renewal, of cleansing and healing, a hard-fought battle which little by little makes a man actually more righteous and worthy of acceptance, a development which refurbishes his will and enables it to collaborate with the divine purpose. But for the mature Luther the rigorous phrases of St Paul meant something more sudden and more dramatic, a more amazing work by Christ, though one less flattering to man. In Luther's expressive phrase man is justified 'not by pieces but in a heap'; not through any gradual transformation, but all at once by the imputation—the reckoning to his credit—of a righteousness and a pardon earned solely by the work of Christ. With one glorious gesture Christ cloaks man's sin even while man yet remains a sinner. A man is instantly justified when by faith (itself purely God-given) he appropriates this imputed and wholly unearned righteousness. Justification is thus wholly 'extrinsic': it comes wholly from outside man. For Luther himself this interpretation of St Paul solved not merely an intellectual but a spiritual problem: in it he discovered a new sense of hope, trust and confidence. Faith was not primarily intellectual assent to doctrinal formulae; rather was it *fiducia*, a childlike trust in the divine mercy. Its coming should leave a man no mere wistful suppliant, no pilgrim with the long road still ahead, but rather a joyous, trustful child of God, confident in victory already won on his behalf.

Of course, this highly Christocentric interpretation exposed Luther to the charge of antinomianism, but not for a moment did he intend to disparage good works. These he regarded as the quite inevitable results of justifying faith, yet to the work of salvation they contributed in his view precisely nothing. He did not wholly jettison Augustine's slow process of cleansing; this process he identified with St Paul's term 'sanctification'. It occurred as a separate and secondary process in a soul already justified by faith in Christ's saving work, yet it added nothing to that work. A few theologians, including certain Catholics, have lately stressed the smallness of the gap between the

22 Christocentric religion, from which pope, monks and Aristotelians avert their faces; Holbein's woodcut *The Light of Christ* (1520)

Augustinian-Catholic and the Lutheran concepts of justification. Yet from the sixteenth century to our own day this distinction between the forensic and the ethical interpretations of St Paul, between the extrinsic and the intrinsic, has been regarded by most theologians as one of the higher barriers between Catholicism and Protestantism. Whatever Luther may have derived from the *devotio moderna*, the Catholic Reformation was its more legitimate heir. The imitation of Christ lay at the heart of revived Catholicism. For Luther, however, man could not rise even to this lame cross-bearing in the steps of Christ: all the cross-bearing had been done for man by Christ in an unrepeatable sacrifice.

By 1520 it became clear to the world that Luther was adopting several other positions quite unacceptable to the conservative senior generation of theologians. He saw the sacraments themselves as chiefly concerned with the maintenance of faith in their recipients. He reduced them from seven to three, and soon afterwards to the biblical two: baptism and the eucharist. He denied that each Mass was in any sense whatever a repetition of Christ's sacrifice; he also denounced transubstantiation as an Aristotelian doctrine made obligatory a mere three centuries earlier by the Lateran decree of 1215. Nevertheless, he continued to insist on a real presence of Christ's glorified body, coexisting with the substance of the consecrated bread and wine. This teaching—usually miscalled consubstantiation—he stubbornly defended against the bare symbolic interpretation of the rite maintained by Zwingli. In consequence the Marburg Conference of 1529 saw the Swiss and the Saxon Reformations

23 The priesthood of all believers. Those in the boat of the Protestant Church are

fail to build a political alliance. While most modern commentators find the matter of justification more significant than that of the eucharistic presence, it should not be forgotten that the great majority of Protestant martyrs went to the stake over the latter issue. Transubstantiation became the great shibboleth not solely from its inherent capacity to arouse emotion but also because it had been so long challenged by medieval heretics.

Another very significant division arose over Luther's doctrine of the priesthood of all believers. This notion did not, of course, preclude an ordained ministry, but it struck at the Catholic concept of an Order of priesthood set apart by indelible and sacramental characteristics from the rest of mankind, an Order having sacred mediating functions as between God and man. Radical in character, this attack had a natural appeal to the laity, especially when accompanied by more positive ideas of congregational fellowship and by

laymen, holding the Bible; from a painting of 1614

extended public education aimed at enabling all men (and even women!) to read the Bible for themselves. From this stage onwards Catholic reformers were faced by intensified forms of the old problem of anticlericalism. They too had to ask how far Catholicism could also make laymen and laywomen feel themselves first-class citizens of the Church. An aspiring laity was also flattered by Luther's well-meant but unduly venturesome phrases of 1520, which seemed to demand a complete spiritual freedom for every Christian. 'Therefore I declare that neither Pope nor bishop nor any other person has the right to impose a syllable of law upon a Christian man without his own consent.' Needless to insist, these statements were soon qualified when in the Lutheran territories sacerdotal authority was replaced by that of the Bible—as interpreted by the Reformers—and when the corporate life and liturgy of the churches were reorganized by commissions of divines and laymen authorized by princes.

43

Luther and his great systematizer Calvin were biblical theologians: the strength of their case, which had to be met by their Catholic rivals, lay in a thoughtful if prejudiced appeal to the documents of early Christianity. From this standpoint they rejected what they held to be mere accretions to the Christian Gospel. They repudiated the over-biblical Anabaptists who sought to re-create a precise and literally minded discipleship. They also repudiated the under-biblical Spiritualists, for these took the Bible as a mere approach-road to a truth which in the last resort must be revealed by the light within the heart of the true believer. Soon, however, the Evangelical (Lutheran) and Reformed (Calvinist) Churches found their original enemy stronger than the dreaded sectarians. Their main struggle was still with a Catholic Church headed by the Papacy. And despite the mediating efforts of men like Melanchthon and Contarini, Luther's rejection of Catholicism had occurred on too great a scale to allow much chance to ecumenists on either side.

The points at issue did not merely involve intellectual theology. Once accepted in Luther's spirit, the biblical religion exploded a host of established institutions: pardons and indulgences based on the doctrine of purgatory; prayers and tributes to saints; the multiplication of requiem Masses; clerical celibacy; dual standards as between clergy and laity, between monks and non-monks; the notion that souls could be saved by bodily mortification. Quite apart from the more exalted problems of justification and the sacraments, the Catholic defenders had to decide which of these more marginal beliefs and practices could be justified and retained. Some intelligent and eminent Catholics did not lack a critical eye for unscriptural accretions; some were unprejudiced enough to see, and to say openly, that a suggestion or criticism was not automatically invalidated simply because it had been made by Luther or some other Protestant. Yet under the harsh polemical conditions of that century—conditions for which the Protestants must bear a large share of responsibility —it soon became hard to preserve even this limited degree of detachment.

IV EARLY CATHOLIC REFORMERS
AND CHAMPIONS

Historians of the Catholic Reformation have rightly assigned a prominent place amongst its forerunners to Cardinal Ximenes (Jiménez de Cisneros, 1436–1517), the Franciscan who after many years of intense austerities reluctantly accepted in 1492 the office of confessor to Queen Isabella, and three years later the primatial see of Toledo. The latter was not only the richest in Europe but carried with it the high chancellorship of Castile, which kingdom Ximenes administered between the death of Isabella in 1504 and the arrival in 1517 of the young Charles of Habsburg, heir to the Spanish kingdoms. Ximenes thus appears not solely as a great churchman but a very monument to that integration of church and state so characteristic of Spain. Like so many Spanish prelates, he proved far from subservient to Rome; he did not, for example, shrink from condemning the indulgences issued to help the rebuilding of St Peter's.

When a Bull of 1494 empowered the Spanish monarchs to reform the friars and nuns within their kingdom, they naturally entrusted the task to Ximenes. He began with his own Order and had virtually reduced it to strict observance by 1506; some of the results were already visible as the Franciscans began their missions to the Indies. From his own resources the archbishop founded the university of Alcalá (Latin: *Complutum*), his main objective being the better education of clerics. Welcoming foreign scholars and the methodology of biblical humanism, he helped to create that group of Spaniards who were later to become suspect through embracing Erasmian and liberal tendencies. In the academic field Ximenes stood among the progressives. In his day the issue lay between the 'trilingual' universities and colleges (Alcalá, Utrecht, Wittenberg, Leipzig, Heidelberg, Fisher's colleges at Cambridge, and Corpus Christi at Oxford) and the superstitious adulators of the Vulgate text, who suspected Greek as the language of heretics and Hebrew as that of the despised Jews. In teaching and in textual scholarship Ximenes made full use of eminent Jewish converts, whose availability gave Spain such outstanding advantages in the Hebrew and Aramaic fields. He financed the princely Complutensian Polyglot in six folio volumes, the prime monument of early Spanish humanism. The Old Testament in particular forms a *tour de force* not merely of scholarship but of the printer's art. On each page the Vulgate Latin stands in the place of honour between the Hebrew and the Septuagint Greek. With something like a grim sense of humour one of the prefaces remarks that even as Christ was crucified between two thieves, so the Latin Church stands between the Synagogue and the Greek Church. Across the foot of the page runs the Chaldee paraphrase, while Hebrew and Chaldee roots appear in the margin. Begun in 1502 and printed between 1514 and 1517, the Polyglot was licensed by Leo X only in 1520 and came into general circulation in 1522, the same year as Luther's New Testament and six years after the Greek Testament of Erasmus.

24 Ferdinand and Isabella, accompanied by Cardinal Ximenes, enter Granada in triumph; relief by a Burgundian artist (*c.* 1521) in the Chapel Royal, Granada

25 Pedro Berruguete represents St Dominic persecuting the Albigensians, but the spirit and properties are those of the contemporary (1500) Spanish Inquisition ▶

The accompanying policy of racial and religious persecution was not initiated by Ximenes, though he continued it with entire conviction. From her rather lurid childhood experiences at the court of her strange half-brother Enrique IV, Queen Isabella herself retained an unattractive but intelligible hatred against the Moorish and Jewish influences which had then beset the monarchy of Castile. From 1483 to his death in 1498 her inquisitor general Tomás de Torquemada directed his chief efforts against the *moriscos* and *conversos* (respectively Moorish and Jewish converts to Christianity) and may have burned some two thousand victims. The dark reputation gained thenceforth by the Spanish Inquisition must of course be viewed against the background of a crusading Spain and an intolerant Europe. Though few governments pursued heresy with such systematic efficiency, the great majority of educated Europeans accepted the death penalty for persistent heresy, while both interrogation under torture and witch-burning were intermittently practised in almost all countries. The offence especially characteristic of Spain and Portugal would seem to lie not in cruelty and intolerance as such, but in the sinister racialism which assumed that purity of doctrine went with 'purity of blood' and that it could hence be ensured by genocidal policies. The rise of the Inquisition was not in fact unattended by domestic resistances. During the years 1484–7 the freedom-loving Catalans bitterly opposed its introduction by King Ferdinand, yet despite some misgivings in Rome he and Isabella established the Holy Office not only in their Spanish kingdoms but also in Sicily, Sardinia and the Indies. Following various local campaigns against the Jews, a general order for their expulsion was issued in 1492, when the Jewish army contractors were no longer needed for the war against the Moors. There seems little doubt regarding the untoward material effects of this step: one Spanish scholar recently went so far as to assert that the Jews were 'the only citizens of economic ability' and that their flight 'sealed the fate of the Castilian empire before it was born.'

Attaining high influence in this same year of triumph, Ximenes soon sought to assimilate the Moors, whose retention of Islamic culture and beliefs seemed to sully the mantle of orthodoxy. He

26 Frontispiece and Old Testament page from the Complutensian Polyglot; its arrangement is explained above, p. 46 ▶

found himself hampered by a peace settlement of unusual liberality, since the Moors had been promised freedom of worship, dress and education, the administration of Moslem laws by their own judges, the enjoyment of their property and a guarantee that taxation would not be raised. Between 1493 and 1507 the archbishop of Granada, Hernando de Talavera, observed these terms yet made slow progress with his policy of conversion by persuasive methods. When Ximenes increased the pressure and burned Islamic books, there came the revolts which enabled the government to cancel its undertakings and offer the Moors a choice between baptism and exile. The final acts of the tragedy were delayed until the reigns of Philip II and Philip III, yet it was Ximenes who sacrificed not only the dictates of mercy but the one real chance to achieve a solution other than that of the sword.

This hasty intolerance preceded an actual revival of the crusade, for in 1509–10 he led expeditions against Oran, Algiers and Tripoli. Like his contemporary Julius II, the great cardinal came to relish the smell of gunpowder, and his African exploits seemed at the time far more important than the voyages of Columbus. On the other hand his policy, though closely linked to the Catholic Reformation, cannot be said to provide a balanced sample of its attributes. As with all policies involving religious persecution and warfare, the state became the dominant partner and religious aspirations tended to become bound to its chariot. The later career of Ximenes belongs chiefly to the history of the Spanish state. In Spain the secular and the sacred could all too easily become intertwined in a naïve popular exaltation which seldom paused to isolate and analyse the actual contents of the Christian Gospel. Of all the medieval legacies left to the Counter Reformation, the most striking and the most ambivalent was the whole medieval history of the Spanish kingdoms.

During the lifetime of Ximenes the reforming spirit of Europe was far from being limited to the critical and devotional literature we have hitherto examined. There existed also a number of practical minds among the bishops and senior clergy, even though their efforts were little co-ordinated and their successes merely local. In France the clerical representatives in the States-General of 1484, the Provincial Council of Sens in 1485, and the General Assembly of French clergy in 1493 all denounced abuses and maladministration in the Church. The responses of bishops to such pleas usually took the inadequate form of attempts to discipline the religious Orders. At the demand of Louis XII, Cardinal Georges d'Amboise (d. 1510) received in 1501 sweeping legatine powers from Alexander VI, and he did not hesitate to send parties of armed men to expel recalcitrant monks from Saint Germain and to arrest defiant Franciscans in Paris. Like Henry VII in England, d'Amboise extended his powerful favour to the Observant movement among the Franciscans. Meanwhile, in both countries there developed small but influential groups of intellectual upper clergy refined by Christian humanism and by a piety closely related to the *devotio moderna*. If these men were 'Reformers before the Reformation', they were also Erasmians before Erasmus, and they saw their immediate task as the education of the clergy.

In Paris the group centred round the Netherlander Jean Standonck who in 1499–1502 reorganized the Collège de Montaigu and made it the headquarters of a community dedicated to the formation of the priesthood: he subsequently founded other communities in Cambrai, Valenciennes, Malines and Louvain. Standonck was a mystic deriving from the Netherlandish *devotio* and the Brethren of the Common Life; his movement has great interest as an intermediate stage between the educational efforts of the Brethren and those of the Jesuits. It followed the former and anticipated the latter in making classical education the handmaid of religion; it called for a new generation of priests 'who will be taught to embrace mortification and virtue together with knowledge, whose learning will be proved by their lives'. In England a very similar ideal was enunciated by Colet and his group. There appeared to such observers a very real connection between a fluent reading knowledge of Latin and a disciplined life. Without Latin one could not study; without study one could not create the mental world and the dedicated outlook of the true priest. Yet without this interior world, built for priests by the Church through the ages, the secular cleric would succumb all too easily to the worldly activities and sordid pleasures which surrounded him.

There are obvious parallels between the circle of Standonck and that of John Colet, but the Christian humanism of the latter was more specifically centred upon the reinterpretation of the Bible. In 1496–7 Colet returned from Italy and in his famous Oxford lectures on St Paul's *Epistle to the Romans* applied humanist criticism to the New Testament, thrusting aside allegorical interpretation and seeing St Paul in a real historical context. More boldly still he contrasted the apostle's call to conversion with the vulgar emphasis upon external

27 St John Fisher, after Holbein

ceremonies, the voluntary giving of Paul's congregations with the hard-faced exactions of modern churchmen. When Colet had become dean of St Paul's, his sermons were heard with approval by Lollard hearers, and he was suspected of heresy by his diocesan, Bishop Fitzjames. For all that, he remained a Catholic reformer until his death in 1519. He did not depart from orthodox sacramental doctrines; he protested against papal abuses but not against the papal headship of the Church. Unlike Luther, he still believed that man, duly aided by grace, could contribute towards his own salvation. Yet while in France the bishops gave limited encouragement to the disciplinary and educational movements, in England the stodgy episcopate made little response to the pleas of Colet and his friends. It consisted largely of conservative and legally minded former civil servants, promoted at the behest of that pious utilitarian King Henry VII. The most notable exception, the saintly John Fisher, had little scope to inaugurate a national movement, for his diocese of Rochester was among the smallest and poorest in the kingdom. The lump of the national Church was not leavened by the rise of Wolsey, for despite his sweeping legatine powers, the English cardinal proved a less effective reformer than d'Amboise in France.

Meanwhile in republican Florence Savonarola's call to repentance and amendment of life had led the mercurial citizens to make bonfires of vanities and works of art. Yet within a short space of time his enterprise foundered upon the perilous rocks of Italian and European politics. Defying Alexander VI, openly appealing to France and other foreign powers to cleanse the stables of the Vatican, Savonarola stood exposed to the hazards of the party struggle within the Florentine *Signoria*, and on the accession to power of his enemies in 1498 he was soon silenced and sent to the stake. That he did not vanish without trace may be seen in the later works of Botticelli, in the recollections of many thoughtful Italians, in the tenacity of that republican tradition which he had done so much to preserve in Florence. While amid the Italian ferment Savonarola's message could not immediately be translated into practical reforms, within some thirty years a number of Italian bishops were working vigorously to improve the state of their dioceses.

Of these reformers the most vigorous and influential was Gian Matteo Giberti, bishop of Verona from 1524 to 1543. His strong aspirations to the contemplative life had survived even a long period of curial service under Leo X and Clement VII. After the sack of Rome in 1527, he at last gained Clement's permission to withdraw to his diocese, and, even allowing for the enthusiasm of his biographers, it is clear that he had transformed the local situation by the

28 The model Catholic prelate,
Gian Matteo Giberti,
bishop of Verona

time of his death. While he did not neglect the religious houses, Giberti saw that the chief mission of a diocesan bishop must be to his parochial congregations. He did not, like so many prelates, issue orders and leave them to be disregarded: he ceaselessly toured the parishes to ensure that they were obeyed; he expelled ignorant holders of benefices, forced non-residents to return to their cures, interrogated laymen on the needs of their churches, relieved the distress of the peasantry, founded orphanages and almshouses, appeased the local factions which were the bane of social life throughout Italy. Above all, he laid stress upon parish worship in all its dignity and sense of congregational brotherhood. This revival of parish life naturally centred upon the Mass, and it was Giberti who established a Confraternity of the Blessed Sacrament, the forerunner of similar bodies elsewhere. Like his friend and adviser Gian Pietro Caraffa and many other leaders of the revival, he had notions which appear today quite puritanical. He ceaselessly strove to promote able preachers of the Gospel, castigated vain and worldly choir-singing, removed all women from the presbyteries, even the sisters and nieces of the parish priests. Severe with slack clergymen, he was even severer with himself, living a life of toil and frugality which formed a standing reproach to the conventional prelates of that day.

No example was more widely followed by the new generation of bishops. Giberti's methods and liturgical practices were to be imitated by St Charles Borromeo and many other admirers; his printed regulations for parish priests reappear in certain decrees of the Council of Trent. Italian bishops were indeed very numerous, yet it would not be difficult to cite thirty diocesans who, even before the close of the Council of Trent, are known to have resided regularly and set sound examples of pastoral devotion. Of course, few matched Giberti's heroic energy, and an example more broadly characteristic of the changing age appears in Cardinal Jacopo Sadoleto. Like Giberti, Sadoleto had done long service as a leading curial official: indeed, he knew the Curia only from the inside until he was fifty. Essentially a man of letters, he seemed cast in much the same mould as his worldly friend Bembo. He began to see the problems of the Church in far better perspective when in 1527 he at last

29 Cardinal Jacopo Sadoleto, bishop of Carpentras, ecumenically minded humanist and trusted adviser of Paul III

went to reside in his Provençal diocese of Carpentras. Henceforth if summoned by the pope he revisited Rome briefly and reluctantly. In his see, so near the place of Petrarch's romantic exile, the kindly Sadoleto found peace for study and thought, but he also developed a sense of mission and pastoral responsibility which enabled him to stand not unworthily alongside Contarini, Morone, Caraffa and Pole in the major tasks of ecclesiastical reform. As with so many bishops, his autonomy was never complete, since he needed papal patronage to feed the horde of spongers and relatives who then surrounded any such magnate. His labours to turn himself into a theologian were not, judging by the published results, brilliantly successful. His life was gentle and benevolent rather than strenuous. During the summer he would suspend even literary activities and retire to a cool rural haven in the convent of S. Felice. From May to October, he writes to Contarini, one cannot seriously work amid the scorched fields of Provence; learned leisure must give way to idleness, *otium* becomes *otiositas*. This saying one identifies as a reference to Petrarch, yet it was well for the Catholic Church that she produced men of fiercer temperament to oppose the superhuman energies of Luther.

55

In their concern with the new religious Orders, especially with the Society of Jesus, historians of the Counter Reformation have too often neglected the many scholars and writers who individually opposed the Protestant revolt from its earliest days. Sensing without delay the full measure of the challenge, yet receiving little effective help from the official leaders of the Church, these men zealously sought to distinguish the points of divergence between schismatic and traditional theology. In Germany it was their misfortune to be saddled at the moment of Luther's emergence with the obloquy resulting from the Dominican persecution of Reuchlin. Their more lasting misfortune was that they failed to produce from among their number a single writer whose literary genius and popular appeal could remotely match those of Luther. Of the publicists ranged against him, the most able was his adversary at the famous Leipzig disputations of 1519: Johann Eck, professor of theology at Ingolstadt from 1510 until his death in 1543.

In the popular biographies of Luther, Eck treads the stage as a vainglorious dialectician, a beer-swiller of florid countenance and implacable disposition, one who toiled without pause or rest to bring about Luther's excommunication. He was indeed among those who developed a remarkably sensitive nose for heresy, and he went so far as to attribute that of the Beghards to the mystic Tauler. Yet these characteristics are but one facet of a figure not lacking in a certain rough-hewn grandeur. Eck should not be thought a crude reactionary. He was well furnished with humanist learning and his early commentaries on Aristotle and Petrus Hispanus can show something like hostility toward scholastic theology. Five years before his clash with Luther, Eck had aroused interest throughout the universities by a forward-looking attack upon the traditional theories of usury. He boldly defended a return on capital up to five per cent, long anticipating the alleged Protestant support of big business. His good sense and realism should surprise no one, since virtually all Europe's chief centres of high finance developed and remained throughout the century in Catholic countries. In 1521 he published a work in three books *On the Primacy of Peter against Luther*, in 1525 his *Enchiridion*, a systematic refutation of Lutheran theology destined to go through ninety-one editions by 1600, and to be translated into several languages. While he refused to join the ecumenical group which sought an accommodation with Melanchthon, he nevertheless had the intelligence to compete with Luther's offer of the vernacular Scriptures, and in 1537 he published a German Bible for the use of Catholics.

Another champion who risked competition with Luther in one of Luther's own idioms was the talented Franciscan Thomas Murner. A disciple of Brant, he launched a bitter attack *On the Great Lutheran Fool* (1522), mercilessly flaying Protestant excesses and heaping scurrilous abuse upon Luther in person. From such opponents Luther's notorious violence of language naturally attracted much counter-violence: but the one most successful in making the mud stick was Johannes Cochlaeus, who began literary life more gently, as humanist, Platonist and anti-scholastic. Engaged in controversy with the Wittenberg Reformers as early as 1521, he did not publish until 1549 his *Commentaries on the Acts and Writings of Martin Luther*.

30, 31 Left, title-page of a work (1530) against Zwingli by Eck. Right, Thomas Murner displays the folly of the iconoclast in his satire *On the Great Lutheran Fool*

REPVLSIO AR ·
TICVLORVM ZVVINGLII
Cęſ.Maieſtati oblatorum.

Iohanne Eckio authore
1 5 3 0
In Iulio

Sub Reuerendiſſimi patris & ampliſſimi prin-
cipis, D. Erhardi S, R, E. Cardinalis ac
Leodieñ Epiſcopi Patrocinio.

Der.xiiij.buntgnoß.
Von anzögung ſpötlicher dienſt/ſo wir ietz
den heiligen beweiſen.

Eß ŵ il ietz von den heiligen ſagen
Von irem leben in iren tagen

From this source derive most of those stories about drunkenness, immorality and devil-worship which did heavy duty among Luther's critics until finally demolished by Boehmer and other scholars early in our present century. Cochlaeus, a canon successively of Mainz, Meissen and Breslau, attended many conferences and disputations, but he seems in fact to have been little regarded by the Catholic leaders of his own day. It would be pleasant to imagine that the tactics of such polemical writers did little to sway their readers: pleasant but unrealistic, for unscrupulous exaggeration was then an accepted and admired feature of controversial writing.

In France the outstanding early opponent of Luther was the Fleming Josse van Clichtove (d. 1543), for some time a disciple of Lefèvre and an enthusiastic editor of Italian humanist educational treatises. A professor of Paris and canon of Chartres, he soon identified himself with the Catholic defence, publishing a collection of 180 sermons, several works of conservative exegesis and an able but restrained *Anti-Lutherus* (Paris, 1524; Cologne, 1525). This tireless writer has attracted too little attention from the historians of Christian humanism and theology. His works certainly enjoyed a wide circulation and occur even in the book-lists of obscure mid-Tudor priests in the remoter English provinces.

The origins of Catholic revival in Poland might well have claimed mention earlier in our narrative. Admitting the growing tension between Polish churchmen and gentry, one may nevertheless distinguish several prominent clerical advocates of reform even during the fifteenth century. The earlier leaders of the Polish Counter Reformation appeared immediately after Luther's doctrines had been made public. One was the primate John Laski (d. 1531), who even before 1520 had been strenuously seeking to discipline both the secular and the regular clergy. Another was Peter Tomicki (d. 1535), vice-chancellor of the kingdom and successively bishop of Przemyśl, Poznań and Cracow, who from 1524 was busy refuting Lutheranism at Cracow, the chief centre of the nation's intellectual life. These men supported King Sigismund I in his firm but undramatic stand against heresy. Far from being mere frontiersmen of Christendom, they enjoyed a first-hand knowledge of Rome and

32, 33 Left, St Thomas More, after Holbein. Right, Reginald Pole, exiled humanist and Catholic reformer, who returned home (1554) to lead the Marian Reaction

northern Italy; they were familiar with the various currents of Italian reformism, especially with the aspirations of the Oratory of Divine Love. As so many of their aristocratic compatriots passed through Lutheranism to Calvinism, and later on to Socinianism, there was no lack of resistance among the Polish bishops. Nevertheless, the tolerant spirit of Poland affected both her clerics and her laymen. During the 1530s and 1540s the hierarchy called for a General Council of the Church, yet they urged that nothing should be done to debar the participation of Protestants.

In England a sterner atmosphere developed when the state Reformation of Henry VIII simultaneously burned sacramental heretics and imposed the ferocious penalties of treason upon advocates of the Papal Supremacy. These latter were few in number and were initially hampered by their king's own doctrinal orthodoxy. Among the papalists the very few figures of intellectual distinction included the exiled Reginald Pole and the martyrs Thomas More and John Fisher, who had been long prominent among the adversaries of Luther. As early as 1521 Henry himself had denounced Luther's heresies in his conventional *Assertion of the Seven Sacraments*, which on account of its authorship sold well in numerous Latin,

59

English and German versions. When Luther counter-attacked the king, More took the pseudonym of Gulielmus Rossaeus and published in 1523 a vigorous rejoinder.

The subsequent controversy between More and the exiled Protestant translator and pamphleteer William Tyndale shows neither protagonist in an attractive light. More assumed these tasks from a high sense of piety and duty: he wrote at excessive length and showed a lack of colour and nuance quite foreign to his earlier genius. He could see no shred of sense or virtue in his antagonists, while for their part they believed More hopelessly infected by an episcopate long made dull and reactionary through fear of the Lollards. This much is true, that More's attitude to the use of the vernacular Scriptures is negative and markedly less imaginative than that of his continental fellow conservatives like Johann Eck. As a champion of Catholicism he shines most brightly in his last two works, written when he had decisively parted company with the king and lay in the Tower of London on the eve of his condemnation. The *Treatise on the Passion* is a straightforward, majestically phrased work of edification, but the *Dialogue of Comfort*, though in essence concerned with the problem of pain and the uses of tribulation in the Christian life, has strong contemporary overtones. It takes the form of conversations between two fictitious Hungarians, the wise old Antonio and his uncertain nephew Vincent, as they seek to prepare themselves spiritually for impending invasion by the Turk. But the reader required little intelligence to see that the Turk was Henry VIII, and the speakers English Catholics: 'There is no born Turk so cruel to Christian folk as is the false Christian that falleth from the faith.'

These swan-songs of a noble spirit exerted little influence except during the brief reign of Mary, and later among those few Elizabethan Catholics who made a cult of their great countryman. The *Dialogue* was first printed in London in 1553, and again in Antwerp twenty years later. As for the *Treatise*, More wrote it in Latin, and it was scarcely known to English readers until his grand-daughter Mary Basset translated it in time for its inclusion in More's collected works (1557). Some not dissimilar features mark the effect of Fisher's two books in confutation of the Lutheran heresy, and that

34 Learned ridicule between Catholics and Protestants continued throughout the century. These invectives against the scholar Polycarp (who edited a Protestant history of the Jesuits, 1593) are printed to form an ass and a whip

of his work (Cologne 1525–7) defending the Catholic eucharist against the Swiss Oecolampadius and written in Latin for the learned of Europe. These works were read abroad with a mounting respect on their author's martyrdom, yet they seem to have made little impact on English opinion. As for the brief vernacular treatises written by Fisher in the Tower and addressed to his sister, a Dominican nun, they belong purely to the old ascetical tradition and might fairly be called survivals from the previous century. In this they are typical of their saintly author. Born in 1469 and a decade older than More, the bishop of Rochester thought along antiquated lines concerning church, state and society. His unworldliness and his lingering respect for the Holy Roman Empire involved him in the efforts made by the Habsburg ambassador Chapuys to revive feudal rebellion and civil war in England.

Luther's earlier adversaries thus wrote few masterly or attractive works, yet it remained all-important to the Catholic cause that Protestant contentions should not go unanswered. Most of these men cannot rightly be dismissed as lone medieval voices in a brave new world. Nearly all the early Catholic champions—Eck, Murner,

61

Emser, Clichtove, Cochlaeus, More, not to mention Erasmus himself—had been reared in the humanist tradition. They were not champions of Thomism, and in so far as any common scholastic background existed among them, it was the same from which Luther himself had sprung: the *via moderna* which looked back to William of Occam. So far as concerns Erasmian humanism, its role in relation to the great religious struggles can easily be exaggerated or misunderstood. If we mean by humanism a sceptical, anti-clerical attitude, then it existed long before Erasmus and it continued to grow after his time in opposition to Catholicism and Protestantism alike. If humanism means the application of classical studies to life and letters, then humanism soon became irremediably split by Luther's revolt. After 1525 humanists in this latter sense can hardly be regarded as forming an independent 'third force'; they failed to create a politico-religious party playing any effective role in the confessional battle.

During the sixteenth century humanism was coming to signify the normal up-to-date education, the current mode of expression. 'All the scholars', wrote one of them in 1518, 'are Erasmians, apart from a few skulking monks and petty theologians.' Humanism was now a way of thinking and writing, an instrument rather than a creed, a technique of communication rather than a philosophy or a theology or a plan of action. At least in our modern easy-going use of the word, we have to label as humanists nearly all men of importance during the period 1520–60. It will become increasingly evident that some humanists used their skills on behalf of the Protestant Reformation, while others bestowed them with at least equal conviction in the cause of Catholic Counter Reformation. The eloquence they had acquired through Latin could soon be transferred to the vernaculars when they left their lecture-rooms and appealed to the public. As Erasmus, Luther and even Loyola all discovered, human beings were not theological computers. It was through fluent, intelligible, non-scholastic prose, not through a *summa theologica* or a set of *quaestiones*, that one could win the hearts and minds of men.

V THE RELIGIOUS ORDERS

35 An itinerant monk
from the *Swiss Chronicle* (1548)

To any modern eye monasticism will seem a permanent and vital aspect of Catholicism, perhaps even a barometer of its spiritual prosperity. Yet during the earlier stages of the Catholic Reformation such a view appeared far from axiomatic to many earnest and orthodox leaders of the Church. We shall soon encounter the disillusioned, even suspicious attitude adopted by the reforming cardinals in their famous memorandum of 1538. By this date a widespread revival seems to us distinctly observable among the older Orders, while several new ones had already become conspicuous in Rome itself by their enthusiasm and charitable labours. Yet even the Society of Jesus was fortunate to win papal approval about this time, for still the talk was less concerned with founding than with amalgamation and suppression.

The state of Europe's religious houses during the early decades of the century defies any brief generalization. Some few were marked by spiritual and intellectual idealism, others near by plunged in complacency and sloth, their misfits constantly attracting unfavourable attention. Yet long beforehand at least three spontaneous movements had foreshadowed the coming revival. The Augustinian Canons of Windesheim had begun among the Dutch houses of their Order that remarkable cult of prayer and scholarship which operated at the heart of the *devotio moderna*. Closely linked with Windesheim were the Brethren of the Common Life, laymen and clerics living under a rule but free to pursue their various callings. Long before the Jesuits, the Brethren understood the crucial significance of Christian education; their famous schools in the Netherlands and north Germany nourished a number of famous men from Nicholas of Cusa (d. 1464) to Erasmus. To a marked degree this

36 *The Tree of the Franciscans*, etching by Jacques Callot

combination of an interior religion with a task in the world anticipated what is often considered 'new' in the religious Orders of the Catholic Reformation. Nevertheless, when Erasmus turned against the mentors of his youth he was not guilty of pointless ingratitude. The Brethren and the *devotio* in general had inherent weaknesses, and after 1500 they tended to lose touch with the new age. Despite its continuing influence upon the interior life, the quiet, Quakerish piety of the *Imitation of Christ* contrasts starkly with the hard-thinking, methodical, argumentative, adventurous, world-conquering outlook of the Society of Jesus. In these contrasts of method and atmosphere lie the reasons why the Jesuits, not the Brethren, broke out of a merely regional background and shaped the Church throughout a world suddenly made vast by exploration and trade.

A second movement of revival dating from the mid fourteenth century was the Observance, a movement towards the rigorous application of the Franciscan rule. It presently extended to the other Orders of friars and compelled each house to choose whether it would join a reformed Observant or a non-reformed Conventual group. The rivalries between these two continued to attract much attention, and Luther himself arose from the Observant wing of the Augustinian friars, then headed in Germany by his personal counsellor Staupitz. Yet, as will shortly appear, Franciscan revivalism was in the last resort devotional rather than polemical.

A third source of vitality was the old and select Carthusian Order, which had never fallen from its pristine ideals, yet had kept abreast of the 'new' contemplative literature. Though some famous Charterhouses, especially those of Cologne and London, exerted a deep influence upon devout lay people, this remained a strictly enclosed Order, its rule based upon solitary meditation. Its network was thinly spread across Europe, and the rural situation of many Charterhouses debarred them from establishing direct contacts with large populations. Yet their indirect influence through notable laymen and through members of other Orders remained a real if somewhat imponderable factor in the religious revival.

Outside these and a few other limited groups, the religious of the early sixteenth century found themselves without much sense of mission towards society. No longer were they bearing the torch of civilization to the dark corners of Europe and too many of them

37 Not a few members of the religious Orders fell victim to vengeful Protestants, e.g. these Observantine friars massacred by Dutch partisans in 1580

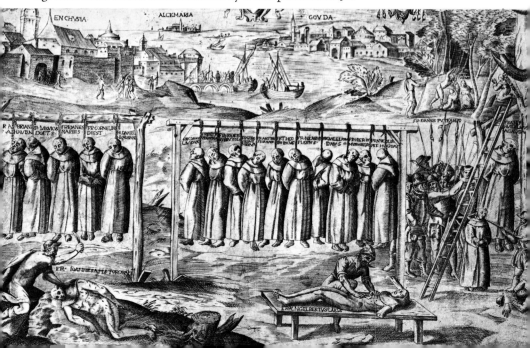

lagged far behind the best standards of lay education and piety. Some found it easy to forget how often in more heroic ages devotional values had been found compatible with outward-turning works of charity. Many communities made their most elementary mistakes by accepting very young novices, imposing inadequate tests of vocation and clinging to the bored and the maladjusted. Even rigorous houses could acquire their share of neurotics and romantics. With or without the knowledge of their superiors, some of the restless brethren obtained papal dispensations from their vows, while others managed to roam around for years with little supervision or sense of purpose. In the universities regular clerics abounded, yet courses were very long and when at last the inveterate students returned to their houses—so many of which lay in remote and boorish backgrounds—they found too little scope for the exercise of their hard-won knowledge. In a world where few parish priests could compose and deliver sermons, the preaching friars remained a most vital agency in the dissemination of religious knowledge. On the other hand, the innumerable lay contacts of an uninspired monastery or friary could tend to debase the religious rather than edify the laity.

In some parts of Europe, especially in France, monastic estates and buildings had by no means recovered from the ravages of prolonged warfare and economic recession. The number of their inmates had greatly declined and many of their heads were mediocrities who had reached their offices through royal, noble or papal favouritism. Even the great Benedictine abbeys in and around Paris—Saint-Denis, Saint-Martin-des-Champs, Saint-Germain-des-Prés, Saint-Magloire and Lagny—have left a massive deposit of records testifying to maladministration and indiscipline. Some of the Orders, notably the Cistercians, had during the fifteenth century passed out of genuinely monastic leadership. The heads of houses were now mostly commendatory abbots, senior secular clergymen appointed by the king and mainly interested in collecting their abbatial revenues. A similar situation fatal to disciplinary reform prevailed in a great number of Italian houses. In the easy-going world of early sixteenth-century English monasticism, some at least of the major abbots were country gentlemen, living graciously and softly in their fine private houses, too withdrawn from their monks, surrounded by grasping relatives and local gentry avid for stewardships and leases. When Henry VIII dissolved the English monasteries, the acute regrets seem to have been limited to those remote areas where their hospitality was appreciated. Among the purchasers of former English monastic lands from the Crown, many men of strong Catholic orthodoxy appear. To the lower orders everywhere the monasteries, as distinct from the friaries, were first and foremost landlords. The monks had often to contend not merely with an exploiting aristocracy but with a restless peasantry. The maintenance of their buildings proved a heavy burden and they could seldom afford striking beneficence. In Germany rich, lordly monasteries furnished prime targets for the depredations of the peasant rebels in 1524–5. All in all, Europe's religious houses were in need of real friends. By embracing fresh concepts of Christian social service, the more enterprising regular clergy of the Counter Reformation were to recover not merely their own self-respect but the respect for monasticism of society at large.

38 *The Devil and the Friars,* satirical engraving from the *Swiss Chronicle* (1548)

At this time circumstances called for new religious idioms, yet they also demanded a co-ordination of discipline which could best be supplied by the highest ecclesiastical authority. The Renaissance Papacy showed itself by no means unaware of the problem. Under Leo X the Lateran Council gave thought to the effect of papal dispensations upon monastic discipline. In 1516 Leo placed all religious persons, even friars, under the rule of the bishops when they were working outside their own houses. The following year he sought to allay sporadic quarrels between Franciscan Observants and Conventuals by a plan to place each wing under a centralized authority. Yet these well-meaning attempts to promote reform from above accomplished infinitely less than did a number of movements arising from laymen, from secular clerics, from the obscurer corners of the monastic world itself. Most of such movements sprang from individuals of marked sanctity and powers of organization, extraordinary men and women to whom no brief survey can do justice. The scope of their activities varied greatly and historians, unlike hagiographers, must seek to distinguish between those who did little more than illustrate a rising spirituality from those others who made large-scale impressions upon the world. Yet the social effectiveness of such movements cannot always be measured by the number and size of the religious communities created. The refounding of the Camaldolese, an old Order of reformed Benedictines, produced a large crop of new houses, but since these were enclosed, their effects upon Italian religion had distinct limits.

More obviously a child of the new age was the Theatine Order established by Gaetano Thiene (St Cajetan, d. 1547) and Gian Pietro Caraffa, then archbishop of Brindisi. The former, a Vicentine nobleman and priest, gave up a lucrative office in the papal Curia in order to combat the decadence of the secular clergy. He and Caraffa were among the first to realize that while old-style monasticism was largely irrelevant to this task, an Order of secular clerics, working in the world but bound strictly to a rule, might well exercise a wide influence. Papally confirmed in 1524, the Theatines maintained a strict rule of poverty, yet being forbidden to beg alms they attracted many idealists with independent incomes and aristocratic

39 Gaspar Contarini, the great liberal Catholic reformer, whose failure and death (1541–2) proved a landmark of the Counter Reformation

connections. Their impact upon the Church as a whole thus proved somewhat indirect, yet as a school for future bishops they eventually promoted episcopal reform programmes, one of the most vital aspects of the Catholic Reformation.

Both the Theatine founders had first been members of the Oratory of Divine Love, not in itself a religious Order but a species of holy club for both laymen and clergy, aimed at personal sanctification and practical charity. As early as 1494 an Oratory of this sort had been founded at Vicenza and dedicated to St Jerome. By 1500 an Oratory of Divine Love existed at Genoa, having been founded by a layman Ettore Vernazza under the inspiration of St Catherine of Genoa. At some unknown date he moved it to Rome, where it attracted into membership several high officials of the Curia. From 1517 or earlier a distinguished group was meeting under this name in the Roman suburb of Trastevere, and soon afterwards it put forth branches in Verona, Vicenza, Brescia and other towns. Though in 1527 its leadership was dispersed by the sack of Rome, it had during this decade brought together a remarkable group of fine spirits, chief among them the Venetian diplomat Gaspar Contarini, who had experienced a personal crisis and conversion as early as 1511, but who was to remain a layman even after his accession to the cardinalate a quarter of a century later. He and some other members like the future Cardinal Morone placed a marked stress upon justification by faith, at all events upon Augustine's version of that Pauline doctrine. In later years they naturally incurred the suspicions of heresy-hunters who feared Luther more than they studied St Paul, yet before Augustinianism fell into disrepute, Contarini and Morone were to be placed by Paul III among the official architects of reform.

Thus deriving from the Oratory, the Theatine concept soon extended to founders and members of Orders which functioned on lower social levels. The Clerks Regular of St Paul—known as Barnabites after the name of their church in Milan—were founded by three north Italian laymen of the professional class. Significantly, their rule included a special obligation to study the Pauline Epistles. Recognized by the Papacy in 1533–5, they soon become famous for their evangelical open-air meetings in the cities of northern Italy, and later on they furnished St Charles Borromeo (1538–84) with valuable help in missions to his diocese of Milan. A further variant on the theme appears with the Somaschi, confirmed in 1540 by Pope Paul III but founded ten years earlier by the Venetian nobleman Girolamo Miani, whose compassion had first been aroused by the

40, 41, 42, 43, 44 Members of religious Orders, as engraved in 1695:

many waifs and strays left around Bergamo in the recent wars. With their hospitals in Venice, Verona, Como and Milan, the Somaschi set an eloquent example of practical charity. In 1547 they became affiliated to the Theatines but, subsequently recognized as a separate Order, they were remodelled in the mid seventeenth century, having then three Italian provinces and a fourth in France.

Another Order distinctly democratic in flavour was that of the Capuchins, reformed Franciscans, who established themselves at Camerino in 1528 and were protected against their Conventual adversaries by Vittoria Colonna, the noble bluestocking famous for her friendships with Michelangelo and Juan de Valdés. They preached and worked among the populace, and in many parts of Italy they undoubtedly did much to bind the wavering masses to the Church. But the Capuchins were fortunate to escape dissolution amid the scandal of 1541, when their brilliant vicar general Bernardino Ochino absconded to Protestantism. This crisis surmounted, they continued to expand, though not until 1619 did they win independence from the Conventuals. At that date they could boast some fifteen hundred houses and they still figure as the stricter of the two Franciscan groups. Their activities in the sixteenth century represented only one of many Franciscan movements.

Theatine; Barnabite; Carthusian; Clerk Regular of the Somaschi; Oratorian

Long before the much-publicized Jesuit missions, the Franciscans had become familiar figures in most of the Spanish and Portuguese colonies. In 1523-4, for example, Franciscan missionaries were in Mexico with Hernan Cortés, and imbuing him with the apocalyptic notions beloved by not a few members of their Order. They assured Cortés that the Church in Europe had sunk into degeneracy, and that he had been chosen by God to establish a new apostolic Church in this uncorrupted land. This vision harmonized with his desire to create a world-wide Christian empire for Charles V, and Cortés took it quite seriously for the rest of his life. Even after his return to Spain, other Franciscans continued to hail him as a divinely appointed agent of the faith. Meanwhile, people less visionary and less naïve were striving to restore the spirit of St Francis in various parts of Europe. In Naples, for example, Maria Laurentia Longo (d. 1542) founded the Capucines, framing their rule on that of the Poor Clares, which three centuries earlier St Clare had received from Francis himself. In Spain the austere mystic St Peter of Alcántara developed from 1556 the Order of Discalced (i.e. shoeless) Franciscans. In turn he was prominent among the counsellors of St Teresa of Ávila, and from the year of his death (1562) his example bore fruit in her Discalced Carmelitesses.

45 Dominican friars valiantly championed the rights of native peoples. The mid-sixteenth-century *Xanhuitlan Codex* shows Fray Domingo de Santa Maria, vicar of Tepozcolula, Mexico, with two of his native flock

46 Paintings by Gaudenzio Ferrari in S. Maria delle Grazie, Varallo, done at the time of St Angela Merici's visits to the church

Of all the new and reconstituted Orders for women, the most important was founded by a saint who remained a Franciscan Tertiary all her life, even as she gathered a company of like-minded maidens and matrons, and framed her own simple but remarkably independent rule. When in 1535 Angela Merici (d. 1540) established the Ursulines she had already for some decades been tending the sick, the poor and the ignorant in Brescia and the towns around Lake Garda. This daughter of a small country gentleman did not leave a single letter of her own and she was unattended by that personal publicity which surrounded so many lesser figures of the day. Born as early as 1474, she was influenced by the practical spirit of the Oratories, one of which existed at Brescia. Yet like Loyola she was slow to conceive her own master-plan. The story of her earlier years goes back to the well-springs of the Catholic Reformation and serves to correct the over-secular image of Renaissance Italy

73

beloved by Burckhardt and his followers. In the quieter corners of that ever-creative land there remained innumerable households where an unaffected Christianity remained normal, where children could be reared in virtue, where from time to time a young saint might grow spontaneously, nourished by local tradition, inspired both by earlier models of sanctity and by their living counterparts among the nuns and recluses. The early influences exercised upon Angela Merici by the older devotees, Stefana Quinzani and Osanna Andreasi, show the powerful continuities within this spiritually stable world. Many sources of the Catholic Reformation may be traced in local history, and here among the lakes and valleys along the northern fringe of the Lombard plain may be observed one of these fertile backgrounds. Here were impressionable little towns, a tradition of social labour among the suffering, a tendency to identify heresy with the hated foreign mercenaries; while northward along the gateways to the Alps the girdle of shrines seemed to pious eyes the outposts of true religion along the frontiers of Italy.

Like Loyola, St Angela deliberately rejected the notion of an enclosed Order. Beginning as spiritual mother of a devoted family, she turned their eyes outwards to human sorrow and boldly sought to convert Italian society. Though her deepest aim lay in imparting Christian instruction to girls, she did not foresee the day when the Ursulines would also accept full responsibility for the secular aspects of their education. In fact, they founded their first school in Parma as late as 1595, but thenceforth they became by far the greatest as well as the earliest teaching Order of women.

Most of these developments in the life of religion came from the heart of the Italian people in that supremely great and versatile age of its history. They were to be followed by one of the most effective Italian foundations, the Roman Oratory under its magnetic leader St Philip Neri. Even so, as in other fields of human achievement, Italy yielded the first fruits of a wider harvest. The Spanish Carmelites we have already glimpsed, and later on there came a plethora of revivals and new Orders, especially in France. Greatest of all, the Society of Jesus was international in its early backgrounds, supra-national in its thinking and in its objectives.

47 Device from title-page of the Jesuit canons (1574)

The transition of Ignatius Loyola (1491–1556) from a military to a spiritual knight-errantry proved no simple act of sublimation. It entailed a broadening of awareness from a remarkably narrow viewpoint to one which strove to comprehend the whole of humanity. It was a harsh process of unlearning and the solution of an inward tension not unlike Luther's, since Loyola also felt his personal inadequacy confronted by the all-seeing gaze of an infinitely pure and majestic God. On pilgrimage to Montserrat, and then living the primitive life of a hermit in a cavern near Manresa, Ignatius failed like Luther to find reconciliation in mere personal austerities. But whereas Luther, a professor of biblical theology, found it in an interpretation of St Paul on Justification, the unlearned but fervent Ignatius found it in compelling visions of God. 'He thought to himself,' wrote his successor Laynez, 'that even if no Scriptures had been given to us to teach us the truths of faith, he would nevertheless have determined to give up life itself for them, purely on account of what he had seen with the soul.'

The vision already attained, a precious decade then passed while Loyola educated himself and sought a true direction for his mission. His romantic dream of converting the Moslem world did not vanish before the discouraging facts revealed during his visit of 1523 to the Holy Land. Learning the rudiments of Latin grammar with the schoolboys of Barcelona, he went on to the universities of Alcalá and Salamanca, preached in the streets and was twice imprisoned by the Inquisition as one of those *Alumbrados* whose false mysticism was then provoking every Spanish heresy-hunter. Significantly, he transferred to the cosmopolitan atmosphere of the university of Paris. Despite the intolerance of its theologians, Paris liberated Loyola and his companions from the local patriotisms which would have strangled at birth the international outlook of his Society.

During the seven years 1528–35 he studied at the Collège de Montaigu (left by Calvin about the time of his arrival) and later at the Collège de Ste Barbe. Despite his Basque tenacity and clearheadedness, he showed no special academic brilliance. Yet from this point he developed a sixth sense for discerning the hidden potentialities of men, and a strange ability to impress and enlist anyone, however reluctant, whose talents he needed for the cause.

On 15 August 1534 six companions climbed with him to the chapel of Saint-Denis on the heights of Montmartre. There they made vows of poverty and chastity, undertaking a missionary crusade in Palestine; and should the last prove impossible, they undertook a vow of absolute obedience to the pope's orders, wherever these might lead. Soon afterwards these six disciples became nine: the Savoyards Pierre Favre and Claude Le Jay, the Portuguese Simon Rodriguez, two Frenchmen Paschasius Brouet and Jean Codure, and four Spaniards Francis Xavier, Diego Laynez, Alfonso Salmeron and Nicholas Alfonso of Bobadilla. In the event, their small numbers, their complete lack of material resources, even their lingering uncertainties of method, were transcended by intelligence and moral qualities of the highest order.

49 Portrait of Loyola (*c.* 1622) attributed to Juan de Roelas

48 Detail of a page from Loyola's spiritual autobiography in his handwriting

To their leadership Ignatius brought far more than a series of heroic gestures: the new society grouped itself not only round the man but round a scheme of devotion clearly embodied in his *Spiritual Exercises*. By 1534 the book was not yet in print, but its text had already matured; it is a strange fact that at least its elements had been worked out in 1522–3 at Manresa before Loyola became literate in Latin. At this early stage he had certainly derived a broad motivation from the *Imitation of Christ*—systematic meditation was very much a characteristic of the *devotio moderna*—and presumably from García de Cisneros, whose *Exercises of the Spiritual Life* had been given him by a French monk at Montserrat. Yet from the first Loyola's own work was neither a *pastiche* nor the artless outpouring of an enthusiast. It was the work of one with a powerful and original insight into the mental habits of devout men, into the well-springs of human action. Even in the perfected form of later years it lacks any very obvious literary attraction and the somewhat disappointed modern who swiftly reads it through should pause to recall that its author did not provide it for this purpose. It is a manual of instructions for those who make or direct a certain sort of religious retreat: an exceptional retreat intended to have a transforming effect upon life and character. It seeks to stimulate a following of Christ which shall consist not merely in mental experiences but in apostolic action.

The *Exercises* are practical and ascetical; they are orderly and very specific meditations around the life and death of Christ. Unlike the mystical directors, who so often bid us cleanse the mind of images, Loyola encourages the creation of vivid and concrete imagery.

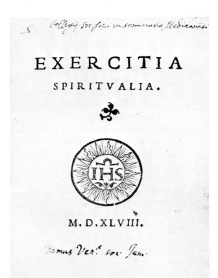

50 Title-page of the first edition of the *Spiritual Exercises* (Rome 1548)

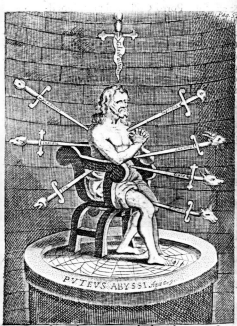

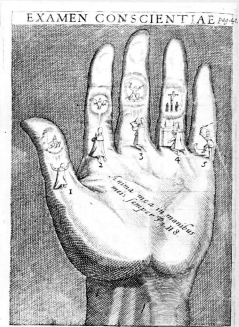

51, 52 Diagrams from an illustrated edition (1689) of the *Spiritual Exercises*. Left, the Seven Deadly Sins; right, the Examination of Conscience

Certain modern writers have in fact blamed this 'new' Jesuit technique of meditation for killing the older arts of mystical contemplation. The charge cannot lightly be brushed aside, since in later days there were Jesuits and others who disparaged the older tradition as a species of Quietism inimical to apostolic effort. Nevertheless, an antithesis so crude represents but one facet of a complex actuality. Between meditation and contemplation there hangs no iron curtain. Several mystics teach meditation as a parallel or preparatory technique. In the work of Abbot Blosius or in the *Interior Castle* of St Teresa, it is clearly the latter. Luis de Granada's deservedly famous and popular *Guide of Sinners* (1555) is the work of a practising mystic, but he also teaches a mode of meditation not unlike that of Loyola,

79

though framed along simpler lines. García de Cisneros (like the *Imitation of Christ* itself) bids his readers visualize the Inferno. That greatest of mystical theologians, St John of the Cross, discusses the ascent from meditation to contemplation and remarks that the process is not always abrupt: it may involve a period of alternation between the two, while some contemplatives may never wholly abandon meditation.

On the other hand it would seem quite mistaken to think of the versatile Ignatius as unilateral either in his practice or his teaching. Towards the end of his *Exercises* the section called 'Contemplation for obtaining Love' certainly deals with the mystical approach. And even within the Jesuit Order itself there long survived a tradition illustrating the compatibility of the two modes. One of the Jesuit mystics was the famous lay brother of Mallorca, St Alphonsus Rodriguez (d. 1617), while later on in France Louis Lallemant (d. 1635) combined a distinguished career in the Society with a staunch defence of contemplative religion against the opposition of his own colleagues and pupils. Again, outside the Society, St François de Sales (d. 1622) drew up a scheme for the devout life which follows a middle path between the *Exercises* and the legacy of the great Spanish Carmelites.

The sheer effectiveness of the *Exercises* as a spur to militant missionary effort cannot be disputed. They can be studied at various depths. A retreat to be 'taken' under a director, they were nevertheless addressed to ordinary as well as to extraordinary souls. Whereas contemplative methods might make an average Christian feel lame and hopeless, the Jesuits came very near to teaching that he might attain perfection not by supernatural graces but in the exercise of his natural capacities. Taken alone, Loyola's dictum, 'I can find God whenever I will', may suggest at least an unwonted departure from verbal caution, but it expressed a deep reality for him and for those thoroughly imbued by his method. His men were no longer mere patients under the hand of the physician. Through athletic personal effort they bent the power of their wills, their senses, their imaginations into what seemed to them an absolute conformity with the divine will. Yet the devotional method and idiom remained intensely

Christocentric. The craving of a troubled but order-seeking century was a craving for precise guidance, and this Loyola offered. When sixteenth-century men read his words, 'The fifth point is a cry of wonder with a flood of emotion', they did not dismiss the system with Benjamin Franklin's sardonic phrase: 'accurate book-keeping'. Within the ordered security of this quasi-Copernican system, the whole potential of a man's will could now be developed, harnessed and projected outward.

In 1535 Loyola's company left Paris for Italy: in 1537 they re-assembled in Venice, where Ignatius and five others were ordained to the priesthood. Had not the Republic become involved in a war with the Turk and their passage to the East prevented, they might well have squandered their lives in a futile attempt to dent the surface of the Moslem world. Moving on to Rome, they encountered there a host of prejudices, partly anti-Spanish, partly directed against their novel advocacy of weekly communion and of sermon-preaching all the year round. Exonerated from charges of heresy, they soon won golden opinions by their service among the poor and the sick during the appalling winter of 1538–9. They also attracted Contarini, that severe critic of easy-going monasticism, and induced him to present to Paul III their proposed charter of foundation.

This venerable document envisages a society of clerks regular, propagating the faith by spiritual exercises, sermons and works of charity, by instructing children and uneducated people in Christian principles. It reiterates the themes of absolute obedience to papal commands, prompt response to the orders of superiors, an absolute vow of corporate and personal poverty apart from the funds necessary to establish and maintain houses of studies. The fifth and last article of the charter proposes the abolition of the choir offices, which had seemed to former Orders the kernel of the religious life. In their first excess of practical zeal, they would, but for the Pope's veto, have abolished all musical services from their houses and churches. Otherwise Paul III heard the articles with deep approbation, and in his growing insight he is said to have exclaimed, 'There is the finger of God.' His Bull of foundation *Regimini militantis ecclesiae* (September 1540) incorporated all the desired principles and empowered the general of the Society to make new constitutions. It also limited the membership to sixty, but little time elapsed before this unimaginative limitation was revoked.

In the following year the election of Loyola as general preceded a swift growth of the Order in striking contrast with the extreme slowness of its gestation. Inevitably, most of the early achievements took place in Italy and in the Iberian peninsula. During these years its membership and ethos were less narrowly Spanish than is often supposed. Twelve years after the foundation the Portuguese members numbered 318, or a full third of all the Jesuits then in existence. The situation in Portugal, with its immense potentiality for overseas expansion, sprang in no small part from the ascendancy over King John III attained by Simon Rodriguez. This mercurial opportunist, whom the king would not allow Loyola to summon to Rome, came near to creating an independent society, and the ensuing problems of discipline and delegation foreshadowed future crises. In those days of slow communications a world-wide organization could not avoid such problems, and they became all the more acute as the Jesuits systematically sought to influence the rulers of Europe, whose ultimate ambitions did not necessarily harmonize with those of the Society. Moreover, from the first its members demonstrated the indomitable character of freedom and initiative in the minds of educated Europeans. Writers satisfied with the superficial clichés have always exaggerated its autocracy and military spirit. That a Jesuit should become *sicut cadaver* in the hands of his superiors represents an ideal of obedience common enough in medieval religious writings: it does not characterize the actual personalities and history of the Society of Jesus. These astonishing early achievements could never have sprung from a system which robbed men of bold initiative or forced them to conform to a type. It arose through the success of superiors in finding suitable tasks for persons of pronounced individuality, intelligence and flexibility of approach. And if in later times the Society lost both prestige and clarity of purpose, this was not due to excessive discipline but rather to a growing individualism which pursued statistical and social success at the expense of profounder considerations.

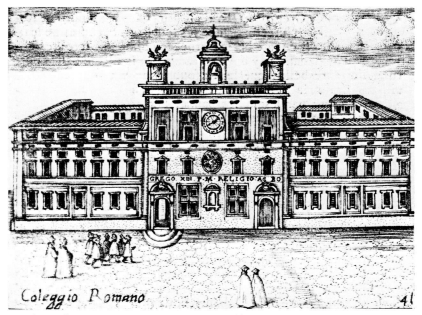

Coleggio Romano

53 The Collegium Romanum; an engraving of 1628

The most tangible gains of the first two decades were those made in Italy. During the 1540s Laynez won much support in Parma before going on to establish houses in Padua and Venice, and to preach (1548) before enormous congregations in the Duomo of Florence. Meanwhile, the preaching of Salmeron made a great impression on Verona, Modena and Belluno, where his sermons were thronged and led to a holocaust of Protestant books. At Faenza, Brouet successfully counteracted the Protestant teachings introduced by Ochino, and at Ferrara Le Jay combated the influence of the Duchess Renée, that leading patron of Calvinism. These and other campaigns prospered not merely on account of Jesuit talents but also through the support of the powerful and the wealthy: the Pope's Farnese relatives in Parma, the Lippomani family in Venice, Padua and Verona, Bishop Giulio Contarini at Belluno, Cardinal Morone at Modena and a number of noble families in Naples and Sicily. The earliest Jesuit colleges appeared in Bologna (1546), Messina (1548) and Palermo (1549). In Rome Loyola founded the Collegium Romanum (1550) and the Collegium Germanicum (1552), which latter became the training school for missions to the disputed areas of Germany, and exercised much influence upon the diocesan seminaries later established for secular priests by order of the Council of Trent. At the time of these foundations the educational policy of the Society was undergoing another vital development. When he wrote his original Constitutions Ignatius was thinking of seminaries purely for his Order. With some initial reluctance he now established mixed colleges partly devoted to non-Jesuit pupils, and he thereby created a means to pervade the ruling and educated classes.

In Spain likewise, colleges were established at Valencia in 1544, Valladolid, Barcelona and Gandia in 1545, Alcalá in 1546, Salamanca in 1548 and Burgos in 1550. Yet despite the Spanish origins of its founder, the Society encountered more powerful resistance in Spain than in Italy. The heart of this opposition lay in the Dominican Order, entrenched both in the Inquisition and in the theological faculties of the universities. Ably led by the distinguished Salamancan theologian Melchior Cano, the Dominicans received much support from royal officialdom and from the Spanish hierarchy. Both these latter were jealously aware of their own past contributions to the cause of ecclesiastical reform, while both harboured distrust towards an organization so clearly devoted to the extension of papal influence throughout Europe. If within a few years the Jesuits won a firm footing in Spain, this was due in large measure to the outstanding qualities of their leaders, to men like the popular preacher Antonio Araoz, that fiery kinsman of Ignatius, and the Estremaduran Francisco de Villanueva, described by a candid colleague as 'a penniless rustic, under-sized, swarthy of complexion, entirely uneducated, vile and despicable in the eyes of men'. Despite these striking disadvantages, Loyola had sent Villanueva to the new Portuguese college at Coimbra, where he met with little understanding from the courtly Simon Rodriguez. Yet once transferred to Alcalá he displayed such obvious sanctity and insight that doctors of theology came to sit at his feet.

At the other social extreme, one of the few early aristocratic recruits was worth a host in himself. Francis Borgia, duke of

54 St Francis Borgia,
general of the
Society of Jesus,
1565–72;
canonized 1671

Gandia and viceroy of Catalonia (d. 1572), was first attracted by
Araoz and Favre in 1541; he sought their advice in order to convert
that great majority of his subjects who were the offspring of Moors
and Jews, and who gave little more than a nominal allegiance to
the Church. Though Gandia is only forty miles from Valencia, he
insisted on founding there not merely a Jesuit college but a miniature
university. The virtues of the future St Francis suggest a triumph of
grace over heredity, since his grandfathers were none other than
Ferdinand of Aragon and Alexander VI! His gentleness and humility
balanced his austere and somewhat naïve aspirations. Under the
orders of Loyola he became a freshman in his own university, and
in 1548, being by then a corpulent widower, he joined the Society of
Jesus. Some seventeen years afterwards he was to become its third
general, in succession to Laynez.

85

Elsewhere throughout Europe the first two decades yielded only modest advances. In France, despite some favours from King Henry II and Charles of Guise, cardinal of Lorraine, the Jesuits were opposed by the Parlement de Paris and the Sorbonne. They attained little apart from the establishment in 1550 of the Collège de Clermont, the house being given them by Guillaume du Prat, who as bishop of Clermont had already been combating Protestantism in his diocese and understood the need for their work. For some years this remained a small private house of Jesuits, but by the early 1570s it was to become an internationally famous college with some three thousand pupils and headed by the famous humanist and theologian Maldonatus. In the Netherlands the Jesuits found a powerful enemy in Robert de Croi, bishop of Cambrai, and even on the accession of King Philip they received little more than tolerance until the mid 1560s. England they failed to penetrate until the middle of Elizabeth's reign, when a hostile government at war with Spain found it easy to depict them as traitors, and all the easier since a few were friendly with men who plotted the assassination of the queen and a civil war. For this late start in England their leaders can hardly be blamed. In January and again in July 1555 when Queen Mary Tudor was seeking to revive Catholicism, Loyola had urged her chief adviser Cardinal Pole to send young Englishmen to train at the colleges in Rome, yet the inept Pole had characteristically failed to respond.

With the threat and then the advent of religious wars, Catholic rulers were in no position to reject such powerful allies, and the fact was most clearly recognized amid the troubled conditions of Germany. As early as 1541 Pierre Favre was attending the Worms and Regensburg conferences with the Protestants, studying the enemy and winning influential friends among the Catholics. He then helped Luther's old adversary Albert of Mainz and administered the *Exercises* to leading ecclesiastics like Julius von Pflug, now bishop of Naumburg, and Albert's coadjutor Michael Helding, later bishop of Merseburg. In 1542 Le Jay and Bobadilla were working in Bavaria, laying the foundations of that future bastion of Counter-Reformation Europe. Five years later Bobadilla was present as an army chaplain when the emperor defeated the Lutherans at Mühlberg, where a thick hat protected his skull from the full force of a Protestant halberd. Undaunted by this experience, in 1548 he strove to dissuade the Catholic rulers from supporting even the grudging concessions offered to the Protestants by the Emperor's Interim of Augsburg.

With the aid of Duke Albert V of Bavaria the Jesuits set up a college at Ingolstadt in 1555 and another at Munich in 1559. By this time their leader in Germany was the Dutchman Peter Canisius. A recruit enlisted by Favre in 1543 at Mainz, he was destined to serve the Society for fifty-three years and to become in its history a figure second only to that of Ignatius Loyola.

Since 1540 the Jesuits had become steadily more aware of the unique importance of the Protestant threat in Europe, yet they did not abandon their old ideal of a world-wide mission. The scope of our present survey excludes any sustained account of their overseas achievements, yet these demand mention, if only as honourable episodes in the ambivalent story of European expansion. This claim is particularly strong as applied to St Francis Xavier (1506–52) and his successors in the East Indies and in Japan. In Goa, which he reached in May 1542, and at the other trading settlements, his mission was in large measure to the unscrupulous Europeans, many of whom, like the official Portuguese historian Barros, firmly believed that Asiatics had no right against Christians. After working in Travancore, Malacca, the Molucca Islands and Ceylon, Xavier reached Japan in 1549: he there entered what he took to be an unspoiled world with no grasping European merchants, no hostile Arabs or Jews to prejudice the people against Christianity. And his words suggest that a people with such high concepts of personal honour had a special attraction for the Spanish *hidalgo* within the saint. Those modern readers who see a noble folly in this solitary assault upon an ancient culture should not overlook some real successes spread across a century. Xavier in fact laid the first stones of a Japanese Church which grew astonishingly until the persecutions of 1596–8, and which survived further attacks until the final exclusion of Europeans in 1640. It was a Church which could boast not merely a succession of great Jesuit missionaries but thousands of native martyrs, some of whom died by crucifixion, a mode of punishment unknown in Japan until, by the bitterest of ironies, it was suggested by the Passion of Christ.

This journey into the unknown had a special quality of heroism scarcely attainable in the familiar landscapes of Europe. Many of the indelible images of the Catholic Reformation are those of Francis Xavier, as he strove to learn languages hitherto unstudied by Europeans, tramped the jungles near Amboina with a Malay hymn on his lips to attract the savages, or walked barefoot up to the knees in snow on his three-hundred-mile journey to Kyoto. At last in December 1552 he died hungry and half-frozen in his wretched hut on St John's Island at the very gateway of his last and greatest objective, China. His was the first and the greatest of the distant Jesuit missions, and whether they followed in his trail or headed for Brazil or the Congo, they did not fail to impress their quality upon European Catholicism. They helped the centre of the Church to

55 Crucifixion of martyrs at Nagasaki, 1597. This etching by Callot dates from 1622, when again numerous Christians were decapitated and burned. Native congregations survived the closure of Japan, some being rediscovered in 1865

56, 57 Jesuit letters from Japan, published 1580 in Italian translation from the Portuguese. Right, a portrait of Xavier when he was in Goa (1542)

emulate the standards achieved on her frontiers, for in Rome and elsewhere the narratives sent back by the missionaries were read with a mounting sense of pride and confidence, as if they had been dispatches from the various fighting-fronts of a world war.

Tied more prosaically to his desk in the uncomfortable Casa Professa in Rome, Ignatius Loyola ceaselessly issued instructions and received reports. Hard on himself and on accomplished colleagues like Laynez and Nadal, he was the essence of courtesy and kindness to the inexperienced and the waverers, to the infirm in mind and body. In such a man Catholic sanctity has shed every trace of the fakirs and thaumaturges beloved by popular religiosity: he looks severely modern and rational, wholly lacking in flamboyance. He took unaffected pleasure in seeing his young men feed heartily, made ceaseless war on dirt and disorder in his houses, insisted on proper medical reports before he would permit individuals to fast.

89

To the end, he had to face the fact that papal and private generosity afforded no more than a precarious foundation for his enterprises, yet he retained an absolute trust in a favouring Providence which time after time seemed to snatch them from the jaws of financial disaster. He needed all his *sang-froid* in May 1555, when the election of his old foe Caraffa as Pope Paul IV caused him 'to shake in every bone of his body'. During these years his illnesses became numerous and the physicians attached no special importance to the one which proved his last. His final recorded words concerned the purchase of a new house in Rome, and he died almost alone in July 1556 before the last consolations could be administered.

Loyola's Society had travelled many long roads from the chapel on Montmartre. At the time of the founder's death it had over a thousand members in a hundred houses, grouped into its eleven provinces: Italy, Sicily, Castile, Aragon, Andalusia, Portugal, Upper and Lower Germany, France, Brazil and India. Yet in the main European theatre of war, its great battles had still to be fought.

58 A device in the Jesuit commemoration volume of 1640, *Imago Primi Sæculi*, showing the dissemination of Jesuits over the world

The process whereby the cause of reform penetrated to the Roman Curia proved remarkably slow. Insensitivity and secularism in Renaissance Rome gave great encouragement to those who saw the only hope of true revival in a General Council. While these 'expectants' included a number of devout and disinterested spirits, many were transparently inspired by political motives. As early as 1460 and 1467 George Poděbrady, the excommunicated king of Bohemia, had aroused widespread interest by his appeals for a Council. The appeals made by various Italians, and by the Venetian state in 1483 and 1509, had been made to embarrass Rome, and made in the knowledge that no experiment so dangerous to Italian interests would in fact be ventured. In Germany some of the universities—for example Luther's Erfurt—were strongly conciliarist, while others as warmly rejected this solution. Above them the Emperor Frederick III had strongly believed that papalism served Habsburg political interests. The true stronghold of conciliarism lay in Gallican France and its chief citadel was the university of Paris. The French kings Charles VIII and Louis XII exploited this demand whenever it helped their interventions in Italy.

In 1510 the French quarrel with Rome came to a head when Julius II deserted his alliance with France, declared Louis his personal enemy and imprisoned a French cardinal in the dungeon of Sant'Angelo. Now in full control of northern Italy, Louis not only gained the adherence of a group of rebel cardinals but summoned the pope and the chief rulers of Europe to a General Council to be begun at Pisa on 1 September 1511. Unrecognized by the rest of Europe, this schismatic *conciliabulum* consisted of little more than a knot of French bishops striving to appear impressive amid the violently hostile atmospheres of Pisa and then Milan. In 1512, as the French military situation deteriorated, they were withdrawn from

59 Maiolica plate
showing the visit
of Leo X
to Florence, 1514

Milan to Asti, and they held their last inglorious sessions across the Alps at Lyons. Meanwhile, in April 1512, Julius had outbidden them by summoning the Fifth Lateran Council, which not only survived the death of Julius but went through twelve sessions before Leo X dissolved it in 1517. Though its average attendance of less than a hundred included few save Italian prelates, it evinced some genuine zeal for reform and may be regarded as a substantial link between fifteenth-century conciliarism and the Council of Trent. The Spanish delegation, while concerned to diminish papal power in Spain and her dominions, presented ambitious proposals which foreshadowed some of the Tridentine decrees. The Camaldolese monks Giustiniani and Quirini produced an even more rousing programme: they called for missions to America, union with the Eastern Christians, rigorous measures to remedy the ignorance of the clergy and regulations to ensure that the laity should receive proper religious instruction Sunday by Sunday. These two Venetians, with whom their eminent countryman Gaspar Contarini had been associated in his youth, placed responsibility squarely upon the popes and boldly referred to the city of Rome as a shameful brothel.

Such documents were straws in the wind, yet at this juncture they failed to assume more substance. Apart from a Bull to prevent simony at papal elections, the decrees of the Lateran Council had little effect upon the Church at large; this mainly because their implementation lay with irresolute popes. A Medici politician, a patron of great art, a devotee of the chase and the theatre, Leo X showed singularly little zeal for the cure of souls. There followed the tragic interlude of Adrian VI (1522–3) and then the second Medici Clement VII, who failed so disastrously to dominate the troubled years 1523–34. In any case, the Lateran decrees concerning pluralities and the tenure of abbacies by non-monastic prelates were so half-hearted, so riddled with exemptions that they could be defied with impunity. The demands of the Lateran Council served indeed to display an establishment in deep disarray. The bishops were not only

60 Clement VII with Charles V, by Giorgio Vasari (1511–74),
Mannerist painter and biographer of artists

ranged against the curial cardinals; they also sought to overthrow what still remained the chief teaching agency of the whole Church: the Orders of friars, whose exemptions so grievously weakened episcopal rule. With much bitterness was this antagonism pursued, and the great Dominican Cajetan said publicly that Pope Leo alone stood between the friars and their abolition. More than twenty measures were passed to reduce the empire of these Orders: they assert the right of bishops to intervene in badly run houses, to examine friars before ordaining them, to consecrate the churches of the friars, to prevent them from dominating parish life at the expense of the secular clergy.

In view of the ultimate establishment of a secure papal monarchy, a real interest attaches to the efforts of Leo X as we see him smothering the threatened eruption of conciliarism and striving to subject future General Councils to papal control. At this time he promulgated the Bull *Pastor Aeternus*, plainly asserting his sole power to call, adjourn or dissolve a Council; he even confirmed the immense claims of Boniface VIII and the notorious Bull *Unam Sanctam*. When giving his vote on *Pastor Aeternus*, he did not confine himself to the usual word *placet* but enlarged upon it with heartfelt fervour: *non solum placet, sed multum placet et perplacet*. About him were arising the glories of Renaissance Rome and when the jarring voice of the remote Saxon friar first reached his ears, it scarcely disturbed the delectable dream.

From this point the chances of a more radical conciliar programme were bound to decline. Throughout the pontificate of Clement VII the moods of the Habsburg and the Valois monarchs increasingly alarmed the pope and his curialists. During this crisis of papal authority the menace of Protestantism was matched, sometimes excelled by the threats of the two great Catholic rulers, each intent to make the pope his chaplain and to exploit the temporal and spiritual resources of Rome. Francis I was prepared in the last resort to stage a Gallican schism, should Clement adhere too closely to Charles V. Henry VIII did in fact stage the Anglican schism when Charles, a nephew of Queen Katharine, forced Clement to block his divorce proceedings in Rome. Following the

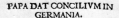

Saw du muſt dich laſſen reiten:
Und wol ſporen zu beiden ſeiten
Du wilt han ein Concilium
Ja dafür hab dir mein merdru n.

Der Bapſt kan allein auslegen
Die ſchrifft: vnd jrthum ausfegen
Wie der Eſel allein pfeiffen
Kan: vnd die noten recht greiffen.

61 Caricature of 1545, attributed to Luther. Left, the Pope rides the German people (represented as a sow), falsely undertaking to grant them a Council. Right, the Pope's theological abilities are compared to an ass's attempts to play bagpipes

great victory of Pavia in 1525 Charles gradually built up a lasting hegemony in Italy, while the sincerity of his Catholicism was offset by his dangerous demand for a German Council to settle the Lutheran problem. In this hazardous situation the prospect of any further General Councils seemed to Rome highly unattractive.

Vacillating and uninspired, the unfortunate Clement nevertheless commands human sympathy as he tries to shake off his allegiance to the Habsburgs, vainly seeks to liberate the Papal States by means of an *entente* with France, sees Rome sacked amid indescribable horrors by an Imperialist army run amok. Above all he failed to prevent either the consolidation of Lutheranism in north Germany and Scandinavia or the withdrawal of England from the Roman obedience. Amid these appalling disasters Clement never bluntly refused a General Council, yet he beheld the prospect with something

95

approaching terror: he even feared to be deposed from his office on the grounds that he had been born out of wedlock, and that his election had been attended by simony. After the sack of Rome, King Ferdinand wrote to his brother Charles V, 'Now you have the Pope in your hands; now the Catholic faith may be restored and a successful Council held.' Yet even for the Habsburgs there soon appeared limits to this form of constraint. Charles had to set Clement free and hope for his compliance, but in the event the devious Medici, profiting from the many entanglements of his would-be controllers, managed to avoid calling a Council throughout his remaining years.

During the vacancy which followed Clement's death in September 1534, Cardinal Alessandro Farnese obtained the votes of the two German cardinals by the assurance that on his election to the papal throne he would summon a Council without delay. So low, however, stood the credit of the Papacy that few observers credited his sincerity. Reared at the court of Lorenzo the Magnificent, Paul III was a humanist, a devout believer in practical astrology, a Roman aristocrat of great intelligence and a man of surprising vigour for his age. Devoted to the Farnese family and to the offspring resulting from his earlier lapses, Paul soon made his teen-age grandsons cardinals, and in due course he elevated his unpleasant son Pierluigi to the dukedom of Parma and Piacenza. On the other hand, his early appointments to the cardinalate also included the saintly John Fisher and the reformers Contarini, Caraffa, Sadoleto, Pole and Morone. This papal Janus, standing as he does between Renaissance and Counter Reformation, imposed delays upon the promised General Council, yet at last in 1545 he called it to Trent. It was he who personally fostered the Ursulines, the Barnabites and the Jesuits; he also took a strong interest in overseas missions and recognized as Catholics the Syrian Christians in Malabar. He enriched the Vatican Library and appointed Michelangelo chief architect of St Peter's. For an ecclesiastic of his age and background, Paul showed a remarkable ability to grasp the facts of the dawning age, and within his relatively long pontificate (1534–49) the foundations of Catholic revival were securely laid.

62 Portrait of Paul III by Pietro Buonaccorsi (d. 1547), one of the ablest of Raphael's disciples

In the summer of 1536 the pope appointed a commission to study Church reform, and its membership did not include a single one of the backward-looking canonists in the Curia. It consisted of the new cardinals Contarini, Caraffa, Pole and Sadoleto, together with the conservative Aleander, the bishops Fregoso and Giberti, abbot Cortese and Tommaso Badia, Master of the Sacred Palace. The report of this commission, called *Consilium delectorum Cardinalium . . . de Emendanda Ecclesia*, was presented to the pope in March 1537. Almost at once its contents began percolating to the public: early in 1538 it was printed without authorization, and despite official efforts to ban its publication it achieved thirteen editions within the next twenty years. In his antipapal bitterness, Luther published a German translation and made much capital from its bold criticisms of Rome.

Nevertheless, the *Consilium* represents an honourable stage in the process whereby the critical spirit captured the Holy See. In a mood remote from that of the Bull *Pastor Aeternus*, its authors began by reproving those former popes who had accepted false principles of papal despotism. The popes had believed the canonists who told them that they owned all the benefices of the Church and could without simony sell what they owned. 'This is the source, Holy Father, from which, as from the Trojan horse, every abuse has erupted into the Church.' First and foremost, the popes must henceforth never break the laws of the Church, never grant dispensations from those laws except by strict necessity, never consent to use their power for gain.

The *Consilium* then descends from the general to the particular. Far greater pains must be taken in the selection of ordinands, since too many of the clergy are at present unlearned, of low background and evil habits. Many are admitted to the priesthood when far too young. 'Hence come innumerable scandals and a contempt for holy orders; hence veneration for divine service is not merely diminished but already almost dead.' The pope should not permit any man to be ordained save by his own bishop or with the latter's authority. In every diocese the bishop should have a master to instruct the lower clergy in letters and morals. Benefices should be granted for the good of the people, not for the profit of the recipient. Italians should not be given foreign benefices or foreigners brought to those in Italy. Benefices should not be burdened with pensions or bequeathed by one cleric to another; simoniacal bargains should not be made on the exchange of benefices. The office of a cardinal is to assist the pope in the government of the Church, that of a bishop to feed his flock: therefore bishoprics should not be bestowed upon cardinals unable to reside in them. At this point the *Consilium* turns upon non-resident bishops and priests, denouncing the exemptions from parochial residence granted by Rome to the latter above the heads of their bishops.

Towards the religious Orders, the critical hostility of the pope's commissioners may seem excessive, despite the fact that many of the regular clergy had still been little affected by the revivals already

98

63 Opening page of the *Consilium* as printed in 1538; Luther republished it with sarcastic glosses. In 1555 Paul IV put on the Index another Protestant edition, giving the impression of a total ban ▶

CONSILIVM
DELECTORVM CARDI-
NALIVM ET ALIORVM
PRÆLATORVM,

De emendanda Ecclesia, S. D. N. D. PAVLO III.
ipso iubente, conscriptum & exhi-
bitum, Anno. 1538.

B EATISSIME pater, tantum abest vt verbis expli-
care possimus, quàm magnas gratias Respub. Christiana
Deo Opt. Max. agere debeat, quod te Pontificem hisce
temporibus ac pastorem gregi suo præfecerit, eamque quà
habes mentē dederit: vt minimè speremus, cogitatione
eas quas Deo gratias debet, cōsequi posse. nam spiritus
ille Dei, quo virtus cælorū firmata est, vt ait Propheta, **Psal. 32. b**
labantem, imò ferè collapsam, in præceps Ecclesiam Christi per te restau-
rare, & huic ruinæ manum, vt videmus, supponere decreuit. eamque erigere
ad pristinam sublimitatem, decorique pristino restituere, certissimam diuinæ
huius sententiæ coniecturam nos facere valemus, quibus sanctitas tua ad
se vocatis mandauit, vt nullius aut commodi tui, aut cuiuspiam alterius
habita rōne, tibi significaremus abusus illos, grauissimos videlicet mor-
bos, quibus iampridem Ecclesia Dei laborat, ac præsertim hæc Romana
curia, quibus effectum propè est, vt paulatim ac sensim ingrauescentibus
pestiferis his morbis magnam hanc ruinam traxerit quam videmus. Et
qm sanctitas tua spiritu Dei erudita, qui (vt inquit Augustinus) loquitur
in cordibus nullo verborum strepitu, probè nouerat, principium horum
malorum inde fuisse, quod nulli Pontifices tui prædecessores prurientes auri
bus, vt inquit apost. Paulus, coaceruauerunt sibi magistros ad desideria **2. Timo. 4.**
sua non vt ab eis discerent, quid facere deberent, sed vt eorū studio & cal-
liditate inueniretur ratio, qua liceret id quod liberet. Inde effectum est, præ
terquam quod principatum omnem sequitur adulatio, vt vmbra corpus,
difficilimusque semper fuit aditus veritatis ad aures principū, quod confestim
prodirent Doctores, qui docerent Pontificem esse dñm beneficiorum om-
nium: ac ideo cum dñs iure vendat id, quod suum est, necessario sequi, in
Pontificem non posse cadere simoniam, ita quod voluntas Pontificis, qua-
liscunque ea fuerit, sit regula qua eius operationes & actiones dirigantur:
ex quo proculdubio effici, vt quicquid libeat, id etiã liceat. Ex hoc fonte,
sancte pater, tanq ex equo Troiano, irrupere in Ecclesiam Dei tot abusus
& tam grauissimi morbi, quibus nunc conspicimus eam ad desperationē
ferè salutis laborasse, & manasse harum rerum famam ad ir. fideles vsque.
Credat sanctitas vestra scientibus, qui ob hanc præcipuè causam, Chri-
stianam religionem derident, adeò, vt per nos, per nos, inquimus, nomen
Christi blasphemetur inter gētes. Tu verò sanctissime pater, & verè san- **Rom. 2.**

A

described. The *Consilium* regards a sweeping reform as urgent, if only because the scandalous state of the monastic Orders sets an evil example to secular priests. The 'Conventual Orders'—i.e. the unreformed Franciscan and Augustinian houses—should be abolished by prohibiting further recruitment. It would be better if all boys not yet professed were to be released from the monasteries. Preachers and confessors to religious houses must be carefully examined by the bishops, while the spiritual supervision of nunneries should no longer be entrusted to monks and friars, but assigned to bishops or other high authority.

While this document is mainly concerned with internal discipline, it by no means neglects the threat of heresy. There are some stringent passages to remind us that Caraffa as well as Contarini was among its authors. Schools and other places of learning must be protected against the many teachers who convey impieties: a clear attack on the free speculation still current in Italian universities. Closer supervision of publishing is demanded. Whereas boys now read in school the *Colloquies* of Erasmus, which lead raw minds into impiety, the use of such books should be forbidden. This rejection of Erasmian satire by prelates who were themselves humanists marks the emergence of a harder policy soon to produce more wholesale condemnations of Erasmus.

A further class of abuses listed by the commissioners relates to the dispensations wrongly issued by the Roman Curia: those granted to apostate monks allowing them to cast aside their habits, to indulgence-sellers who deceive simple folk with their superstitions, to ordained men who decide they want to marry, to laymen who seek to marry within the prohibited degrees, to clerics convicted of buying benefices but still desiring to retain them, to people desirous of alienating Church goods. The final paragraphs deal with the corruptions of Renaissance Rome itself: the swarm of sordid and ignorant priests in the city, the harlots who are followed around by clerics and by the noble members of the cardinals' households, the appalling feuds and factions which call for reconciliation by the pope and the cardinals, the almshouses and charitable trusts in need of proper management. These local criticisms conclude with a bluntly expressed valediction:

64 A genuine papal medal—the smaller one here—had conjoined Pope/Emperor, and on the reverse Cardinal/Bishop. In 1537–47 satirical medals were struck, probably in the Netherlands, including the larger one here: it conjoins Pope/Devil and Cardinal/Fool

'You have assumed the name of Paul: we hope you will imitate the charity of Paul.'

This remarkable document is the work of practical administrators and moralists, not that of theologians or historians. It does not seek to trace back all these abuses to doctrinal or historical origins, and it tells us far more about Rome and Italy than about the problems of the Church in the outlying regions of Europe. It doubtless exaggerates the influence and consequently the blame attaching to the Holy See. It makes too few exceptions; it does not, for example, record that there had always been dutiful, even puritanical cardinals in Rome, or again that secular rulers had contributed much to the mundane mediocrity of the Church. On the other hand, its main criticisms can be heavily supported from original sources of all types throughout the preceding decades. It was doubtless justified in the priority it gave to the task of reforming the head as opposed to the members of the Church. And whereas Luther had diminished the pre-eminence of the clergy and had taught the 'priesthood of all believers', this Catholic programme concentrates upon the clergy as the key to all reform. To its authors the faults of the Church are chiefly those of the hierarchy from pope down to parish priests: the need is for law, order, discipline, above all for the revival of episcopal authority. Rome must not only reform itself; it must refrain from the sale of privileges incompatible with this latter authority. The *Consilium* is a significant Catholic document not merely on account of its frankness or because it foreshadows many of the steps taken at Trent, but also because it thoroughly appreciates the chain of command upon which the effectiveness of the Catholic Church has always depended. It upholds the vital principles then so gravely threatened by the short-sighted fiscalism of the Curia and its agents throughout Europe.

The immediate effects of the *Consilium* fell far below the hopes of its authors and its very frankness hampered its public use. In the autumn of 1538 Contarini adjured the pope to face the loss of some twenty or thirty thousand ducats entailed by a full reform of the Dataria, the office where dispensations and appointments to benefices were issued. Yet a few days later, when Vittoria Colonna asked Paul why nothing was happening, he merely shrugged his shoulders. Intelligibly enough, he shrank from this upheaval and loss, satisfying himself with minor changes which left curial procedures and incomes substantially unaltered. One may nevertheless sense a real change of atmosphere in Rome during these years. In December 1540 the pope found no less than eighty absentee bishops living in Rome and he personally ordered them to return to their duties. Moreover, the more noticeably pious prelates had no longer to tolerate the open cynicism of the Medicean period, and when moral lapses by clerics came to light, pains were now taken to hush them up as matters of grievous scandal.

As befitted men conscious of past errors, Contarini and his closer associates still looked charitably upon those whose protests had meant a withdrawal from the Roman obedience. Yet his hopes of reunion with moderate Protestantism were soon to be dashed. The Lutheran revolt had been in progress for twenty years. It had developed its own ecclesiastical organization, its own liturgical tradition and codes of doctrine, its own spirit of establishment, even its own conservatism, now as hostile towards radical sectarians as towards Catholic revival. And while Melanchthon stood more than ready to talk with Contarini, Luther himself had never mellowed:

his movement was still expanding and he saw no reason to revise his belief that the Papacy lay under God's curse and would soon be deprived of its remaining authority throughout Christendom.

The last significant effort by the Catholic hierarchy to achieve a negotiated settlement with the Lutherans began as early as 1535, when the nuncio Pietro Paolo Vergerio (who later turned Protestant) visited Wittenberg and there detected a continuing disposition to confer with Catholic theologians. The Emperor Charles had the strongest of political inducements to explore even minor opportunities, and he finally promoted the conversations held in 1540–41 at Hagenau and Worms. In April 1541 these were transferred to Regensburg (Ratisbon), where Charles was then holding a Diet of the Empire. Alongside Melanchthon sat the diplomatic theologian of Strassburg, Martin Bucer, together with Pistorius of Hesse. On the Catholic side the detailed negotiations were largely conducted by the theologians of the Cologne school, Johannes Gropper and Julius von Pflug, bishop of Naumburg. These men were Erasmians and moderates, the combative Eck being kept under control by the legate, Cardinal Contarini.

The tragic hero in this brief yet decisive act of the drama is Contarini, whose own spiritual crisis had long ago been resolved with the aid of Augustine's insistence upon salvation by grace alone. In 1516 he had published a treatise defending the immortality of the soul against the doubts of Pomponazzi, and in 1530 a book entitled *A Confutation of the Articles or Questions of Luther*. Though he believed that Luther's extension of Augustine's theology had some roots in true doctrine, and though others constantly suspected him of Lutheran sympathies, Contarini never in fact followed Luther's justificatory doctrine in its more sweeping and original phases. If here his position was not the one later adopted at Trent, neither was it Lutheran. On the other major theological fronts, particularly in relation to the sacraments, he made no significant concessions to Protestant teaching, and he firmly maintained the Papal Supremacy.

Despite some striking initial agreements, the Colloquy of Regensburg cannot in retrospect be regarded as a shot which narrowly missed the target of reunion. Melanchthon's strict instructions were to yield nothing contrary to the sense of the Confession of Augsburg. And though fertile in theological compromise, Bucer himself regarded this meeting as a path towards an eventual peaceful conquest of the remaining Catholic areas of Germany. Among the lesser-known delegates was the young Calvin, still learning his international relations, yet totally and finally convinced that the Roman hierarchical and sacramental systems were based on fallacy. The other side also contained numerous intransigents: even among the German Catholics there were many who thought their spokesmen, Gropper and Pflug, far too pliable. On the political side the first favourable indications did not extend far towards reunion. The most militant of the Lutheran princes, Philip of Hesse, had for the time being joined the emperor to avoid deposition for bigamy. Frederick count Palatine consented to preside, while the trimmer Joachim II of Brandenburg astonished both sides by devoutly attending a Catholic Mass. Yet as a whole the politicians contributed little. Though anxious for a German settlement which did not surrender the essential dogmas of Catholicism, the emperor was at this time sternly persecuting Protestants in the Netherlands. The ostensible Catholic zeal of the Bavarians masked a plan to enhance their own political power by crusading methods. The elector of Saxony, pivot of the Lutheran world, refused to attend in person at Regensburg. And from outside Germany there bore upon Contarini the sinister diplomatic pressures of France. Seeing that an agreement would exalt the power of his Habsburg rival, King Francis persistently attacked Contarini's liberalism, affected to see pope and Church in mortal danger and undertook to wage holy warfare in their defence. Meanwhile, in Rome itself little enthusiasm was perceptible. The emperor had long criticized papal diplomacy, while his control over Italy was bound to alarm any pope who desired to preserve a measure of independence. Moreover, the ardour of Charles to reach a German settlement had always seemed to contain a cæsaro-papalism which might end by creating a German Church free from the Roman supremacy.

The initial agreements at Regensburg covered free will and original sin. More surprising, they also included (10 May) a compromise formula covering a 'double justification' based on Erasmus's *Repair of Christian Unity* (1533) and now acceptable to Contarini and Gropper as to Melanchthon and Bucer. While justification was essentially by faith and grace, dependent on the merits of Christ, nevertheless a justifying faith must be lively and efficacious through works of charity. This position Contarini elaborated at the same time in his *Epistola de Justificatione*. Thirty years later the Sorbonne was to pronounce his version acceptable, yet in 1541 Caraffa and others in Rome denounced it, while in Wittenberg Luther saw the compromise as 'a patched-up thing' and dissuaded his elector from leaving for Regensburg. From this point the parties steadily diverged. Sensing even among Catholics some marked variations of emphasis concerning the authority of popes and General Councils, Contarini left these hazardous problems to the last. Yet he could not profitably postpone a debate upon the eucharist, and here his own unswerving insistence on transubstantiation soon brought about complete deadlock. On this basic issue, the Colloquy perished even before the pope began to express doubts concerning Contarini's formula on justification. Accepting the inevitable, the legate returned to Rome and faced his detractors with a fine serenity. Weary of the long contention, he died in the following year.

His Augustinian and Erasmian standpoint had not yet been universally rejected. The Catholic cause had not been wholly assigned to Caraffa or to the diehards called 'Aleander's four Evangelists': Eck, Cochlaeus, and those two successive bishops of Vienna, Fabri and Nausea. Nevertheless, Contarini's good faith and diplomatic skill had provided no firm basis for negotiation with a Protestant world still dominated by the unyielding spirit of Luther. Devoid of worldly ambitions, deeply respected by the Protestants and sincerely anxious to save their souls, the great Venetian cannot—by any definition which would today seem tenable—be accused of sacrificing Catholic doctrine. Amid a generation ever disposed to lose itself in peripheral issues, Contarini recalled Catholics to the central problems of man's justification, the merits of Christ, the mode by which those merits may be appropriated. That his orthodoxy could be so widely impugned demonstrates both the strength of the Pelagian tendencies bequeathed by the late medieval Church, and the depth of the suspicions aroused by Luther.

The failure at Regensburg and the charges against Contarini were immediately followed by the establishment of the Roman Inquisition under Caraffa. Here in 1541–2 can be seen a major landmark in the transition from Augustinian and Erasmian reformism to a dual policy of reform plus repression. In Spain, however, this transition had been made a decade earlier. The climax of Erasmian influence in Spain had been reached in the years 1527–32, after which a reaction led by the Dominicans and Franciscans had triumphed at court and throughout the country, driving humanists and *conversos* alike into exile. The hardening at Rome in 1541–2 derived in no small part from Spanish examples and counsels. Caraffa himself had been deeply impressed by the Inquisition of Spain while serving as nuncio in that country. His proposal to establish an effective central tribunal in Rome gained warm support from two influential Spaniards there: one was Juan Alvarez de Toledo, cardinal archbishop of Burgos, the other Ignatius Loyola. In the mind of Paul III their pressure was reinforced by an alarming upsurge of heresy revealed in the city of Lucca.

The great powers bestowed on Caraffa by the Bull *Licet ab Initio* (July 1542) were speedily translated into action. Despite his limited means, he bought a house in Rome and at his own expense fitted it with prison cells. Unlike earlier inquisitors, he systematically struck at the highest in the land, while the feuds which riddled every Italian town and district ensured a steady stream of accusations. The persecution spreading thence throughout Italy must be seen alongside similar persecutions in almost every European country. While it claimed a number of martyrs, its main effect was to drive most of the leading Italian Protestants into exile. By 1551 even Lucca had abandoned the attempt to protect its heretics, and in this same year Caraffa secured the appointment of his ideal commissary general of the Holy Office. This was the Dominican Michele Ghislieri, the future St Pius V, the one man in Italy who might be pronounced even more pertinacious and austere than Caraffa himself.

Though from 1536 Paul III was cautiously negotiating with a view to a General Council, this long-awaited assembly did not begin to function until December 1545. The main causes of the refusals and postponements lay in the political configuration of Europe. Faced by the strong military alliance of Lutheran princes and cities, needing help against the Turk, the Emperor Charles still felt bound to negotiate with them so long as any hope of religious reconciliation existed. Even after the collapse of Regensburg he continued to nourish his stubborn hopes. Yet his notion of an ecumenical Council, assembled in Germany and prepared to make concessions to cure the German schism, could hardly be viewed with indulgent eyes in Rome, where the obstinate and embattled character of Lutheranism had become increasingly obvious. In addition, the French did not merely fear a German reconciliation. Confronted by the spectre of a Habsburg-dominated Papacy, the Most Christian King of France stood prepared to back the Turks. The least suggestion of papal-imperial co-operation served to arouse a fierce Gallicanism among French statesmen and ecclesiastics: for many years there continued the danger that Francis and his successor Henry II would imitate the English schism.

On the other hand, many Catholics detected a lack of urgency in the pope's negotiations for a Council; they half believed Luther's insistence on the impossibility of reform, conciliar or otherwise, so long as the Papacy controlled the destinies of the Church. Their unfavourable impressions were strengthened by those long intrigues through which Paul raised the Farnese family to the dukedom of Parma and Piacenza. A pope who carved out for his son a new state from the lands of the Church and who married his grandson to a natural daughter of the emperor must have recalled the Borgias as well as the Medici. Yet aside from his secular ambitions, the intelligent pontiff realized that the Papacy might gain enormous strength

107

from authoritative definitions and reforms promulgated at a General Council. His difficulty lay in ensuring that such a Council, however officially 'free', should in fact be papally controlled and prevented from meddling too intimately with the Curia, the remodelling of which he naturally desired to keep in his own hands. Paul may also be credited with a keen sense of the complexities attendant upon a programme of conciliar reform. Too many naïve optimists supposed a Council capable of solving the troubles of the Church within a few months by the mere re-enactment of old decrees. That the problems of the new age demanded new intellectual activities—for example, researches in biblical theology—became clear to the Catholic leadership only by very gradual stages. Yet in 1545 not even the most far-seeing could have anticipated that the work of the forthcoming Council would stretch across eighteen years, that its actual sessions would occupy four years and produce a body of legislation greater in bulk than the total left by all the previous eighteen General Councils of the Church.

In May 1542 a Bull at last summoned the assembly to meet the following 1 November at Trent (Latin: *Tridentum*), a city within the territories of the Empire yet not too distant from Rome: it was the nearest Imperial city along the great route from the Lombard plain towards the Tyrol. At this time, however, Francis and Charles resorted once again to war, and both forbade their bishops to attend. Additional quarrels arose from the Farnese family in Parma. Moreover, even when licensed to travel, the bishops were slow to arrive, while the lodging and maintenance of their innumerable followers in so small a city occasioned a mass of local difficulties. By the early months of 1543 a very few prelates and ambassadors had appeared, and by July the pope's legates saw no alternative to a further postponement. When at long last the opening session was held on 13 December 1545 it comprised only thirty-one bishops and fewer than fifty theologians and canonists. Except in its final stages the Tridentine Council was never to attain impressive numbers; indeed, it would pass through dark seasons when the spark of life seemed to have fled. Yet with a strange tenacity it would revive and flourish as if protected by unseen powers.

In our modern sense of the term its spirit can hardly be called ecumenical; even within Catholic Europe there existed warring forces which it could not wholly reconcile or balance. Judged by any regional and mathematical criteria, it could not be pronounced representative of Western Christendom. At every session the Italian prelates vastly outnumbered the rest, for in Italy almost every minor city had its bishop. The Teutonic peoples of Europe were represented throughout by a tiny handful of members, while French bishops and statesmen both inside and outside the Council spoke with contempt of its unrepresentative character. Of the 270 bishops attending at one time or another, 187 were Italians, 31 Spaniards, 26 French and 2 German. Of the 255 ecclesiastics to sign the final Acts no fewer than 189 were Italians. Moreover, by the procedural rules adopted in 1545 only bishops and the generals of a few religious Orders could vote in the full sessions. This accorded better with ancient tradition than did the fifteenth-century precedent of Constance, where voting had been by nations and where abbots and theologians had voted alongside the episcopate. On the other hand, the decision of 1545 gave full force to the Italian contingent, very many of whom had small revenues and so depended upon papal grants and stipends.

These rather daunting facts and figures nevertheless demand some qualification. Quite apart from matters of personal zeal and integrity, not all the Italians may be regarded as mere papalists. The Milanese bishops and those from Naples and Sicily can seldom have been unmindful of the wishes of their temporal overlord Charles, while no prelate from the Venetian territories can wholly have ignored the strong antipapal traditions of Venice. Again, the almost negligible weight of German participation should not be ascribed to papal or Italian intrigues. This sprang partly from the natural anxiety of the more zealous Catholic leaders in Germany to remain at work in their heresy-infested dioceses, partly from the fact that many German bishops were the secular-minded sons of aristocratic families, reluctant to mar their enjoyable lives amid the physical discomforts and mental strains of Trent. The grip upon the Council maintained by the popes cannot simply be attributed to a phalanx of subservient

65, 66 Left, Marcello Cervini, pope for three weeks in 1555, commemorated by Palestrina's *Missa papae Marcelli*. Right, Gian Maria del Monte (Julius III, 1550–5) by Scipio Pulzone

Italians. It also depended upon the industry and character of the various legates at Trent. During the first period (1545–7) the experienced Gian Maria del Monte (later Julius III) was assisted by the enthusiastic reformers Marcello Cervini (later Marcellus II) and Reginald Pole. The second period (1551–2) felt the firm hand of the traditionalist Marcello Crescenzi, while the successes of the third period (1562–3) owed much to the Augustinian Seripando, to the brilliant Polish diplomat and controversialist Cardinal Stanislaus Hosius, above all to Morone. With the last Charles Borromeo, the admirable nephew and secretary of Pius IV, remained in daily correspondence, settling the agenda and planning the debates. In Rome also the papal secretaries preserved the records of the Tridentine Council and transmitted them from one session to another.

Despite the changing background and the long intervals, this should be seen as one Council, not three successive Councils. Some of its most effective work dates from its first two periods, and it was the Papacy which secured its continuity and its integration. Another obvious source of strength lay in the wealth of talent made available both in Rome and at Trent, for the Council was no mere gathering of the episcopally beneficed. While the bishops were the official *diffinitores* (i.e. definers of dogma), they had while working in committee the assistance of numerous *consultores*: the expert theologians and canonists, many of them Jesuits and Dominicans. And especially from the last-named there sprang unifying influences deriving from the thought of St Thomas Aquinas, now increasingly accepted as *doctor communis* among the theologians.

Even without the details maliciously supplied by the famous anti-papal historian Paolo Sarpi (d. 1623), it would be possible to select an unedifying picture of the proceedings at Trent. Such a picture would be as little justified as the converse approach which, armed in advance with a Tridentine orthodoxy, ends by seeing in the Council a harmonious assembly of inspired prelates, infallibly guided to the correct conclusions by the indwelling Spirit of Truth. Political interference and national antagonisms obtruded all too often. They were notably strengthened by the presence of lay ambassadors, who not only wasted time in disputes over protocol but were permitted

67 Stanislaus Hosius (d. 1579), Polish bishop and controversialist; made cardinal and legate at Trent, 1561

to state at length before the Council the grievances and opinions of their respective rulers. Behind the scenes these envoys were doubtless able also to stimulate the spirit of nationalism already strong among the clergy. Again, the bishops were concerned to vindicate against the centralizing Curia their claims to a greater role in Church government, claims which aroused tensions perceptible enough even in modern Catholicism. And needless to add, mere personal antagonisms frequently arose. When a Greek bishop accused a Neapolitan of ignorance and perversity, the latter retorted by tearing out his antagonist's beard in handfuls. More typically, unpopular speeches were sometimes drowned by coughing and shouting. Yet alongside the vagaries of a quarrelsome, cocksure and uninhibited generation, there still runs through the Council of Trent an element which cannot be attributed to the mere exchanges of ambitious and opinionated men. A good deal of this eloquence meant what it said; it betokened a genuine fervour, a capacity for self-criticism then rare in ecclesiastical assemblies, a passionate desire to reform and to save the Holy Catholic Church.

68, 69 Left, detail from Titian's picture of the final meeting in the Cathedral of Trent. Above, to cope with increased numbers at Trent in 1562–3, an amphitheatre was constructed in S. Maria Maggiore; the legates and cardinals faced the semicircle, with the lay envoys on their left

113

During its first period (sessions I–VIII) the Council established a precedent of doctrinal conservatism from which its collective action was never to deviate. It found the pope mainly interested in the definition of dogma, the emperor in disciplinary reforms, and hence it decided to treat both matters concurrently. It defied Lutheran teaching quite deliberately when it agreed that Scripture and tradition should have equal validity as sources of truth. It announced the sole right of the Church to interpret the Bible and upheld the primacy of the Vulgate text over all other Latin versions. It did not, however, exclude emendations of the Vulgate and it took no decisions concerning vernacular translations of the Scriptures. It asserted that while all seven sacraments were instituted by Christ and were necessary in general to salvation, not all were necessary to every man. The sacraments actually contained the grace they signified and they conferred it *ex opere operato*, irrespective of the qualities or merits of the persons administering or receiving them. Sacramental doctrines, especially those touching baptism and confirmation, were defined in greater detail than hitherto. Yet by far the most important decree of the first period is the one promulgated in January 1547 concerning justification. By far the longest of all the Tridentine decrees, this consists of sixteen chapters and thirty-three canons. Here the Fathers condemn a number of beliefs, some of them either tendentiously summarized or in fact held exclusively by the extremists or the eccentrics of the Protestant Reformation.

Among these condemned beliefs the following are characteristic: that man is passive under the influence of grace and lacks freedom of will; that good works executed before justification are sins; that nothing save faith is needed for justification; that man is justified solely by the imputation of the righteousness of Christ; that the forgiveness of sins depends on a man's belief that he has been forgiven; that the justified man is bound to believe himself numbered among the elect; that the Gospel commands us only to believe; that the Ten Commandments have nothing to do with being a Christian; that Christ came only as a redeemer and not as a lawgiver; that a man once justified cannot sin or fall from grace; that lack of faith is the only mortal sin. Confusing as it may seem, this list certainly intends to condemn Luther's imputatory or extrinsic doctrine, as opposed to the intrinsic doctrine of justification attributed to St Augustine.

Another decisive action of this period has attracted too little attention: the victory of scholasticism over biblical humanism. In April 1546, during the fourth session of the Council, it seemed indeed as if the latter cause had captured the support of the great majority of the Fathers. Cervini, Seripando, Pole and Bishop Caselli led a strong movement to revise the education of the priesthood and through it the presentation of religion to the laity. Instead of studying the Scriptures in the commentaries of its scholastic expositors, the clergy, in particular the friars, should be led to study the actual text of the Bible in the light of the historical, critical and philological advances made by modern scholarship. The humanist prelates did not expect doctrinal truths to emerge from this re-emphasis, yet they did see Scriptural study as a path to religious conviction and fervour. They bluntly demanded that the Council should announce its priority over the old scholastic disciplines, should largely exclude the scholastic approach from the teaching conducted in universities, religious houses and cathedrals. Suddenly, however, towards the end of May, their initiative was arrested by the powerful pleas of Domingo Soto, representative of the Dominican general: he urged that such a blow against scholasticism would delight the Protestants, who had from the first been urging this same reversal. Amid these second thoughts, the divided Fathers failed either to establish any priority for biblical studies or to encourage the training of more teachers in the humanist tradition. They failed likewise to encourage the laity to read the Scriptures, or to prepare the Scripturally-orientated catechism for laymen which the humanist group had at first confidently planned. This great refusal of 1546 had permanent effects. When seventeen years later the Council came to decree the establishment of seminaries, humanism as a factor in theology had run its course. At no stage did the spirit of Erasmus and Lefèvre suffer a more catastrophic defeat, and in no field did the fear of Protestantism leave deeper marks upon the development of Catholic religion.

Like the rest of the popes, Paul III laid far less stress on discipline than on doctrine; in the former field the Council's work during the years 1545–7 lacks much significance. The ancient canons against the non-residence of bishops were renewed, yet should a bishop be absent for six months without cause, he would be called upon merely to forfeit a fourth part of his annual revenues. As for the lower clergy, they were still permitted 'for reasonable cause' to purchase dispensations allowing absence. The Council applied no check to pluralism, and while in February 1547 the pope himself ordered pluralist cardinals to relinquish their sees within six months, his order was notoriously evaded by most of the offenders.

Having thus embarked upon its tasks, the Council was suddenly thrust into abeyance by a quarrel between pope and emperor. Pierluigi Farnese, whose title to the dukedom of Parma had not been recognized by Charles, now attached himself to France. He also became involved in a bitter quarrel with the Imperial viceroy of Milan, who ultimately in September 1547 had him murdered. Meanwhile, Charles had assumed a dominant role in Germany and had driven the Lutheran forces from the south. He then advanced on Saxony and in April 1547 crushed the Elector John Frederick at Mühlberg. But meanwhile the pope withdrew his contingent from the Imperial forces, while the legates, without fully consulting him, took the excuse of an epidemic to transfer the Council from Trent to Bologna. Furious beyond measure, Charles ordered his delegation to remain at Trent, and in May 1548 he defiantly sought by the Interim of Augsburg to stage a reconciliation with the Protestants. While his terms were far too one-sided to attract the vast majority of the latter, Charles did at least offer them clerical marriage and communion for the laity in both kinds, a gesture bound to cause great consternation in Rome. So matters still stood when in November 1549 the death of Paul III was followed by the election of the legate del Monte as Julius III.

A nepotist and a lover of art, the new pontiff by this time lacked any passionate concern for reform. Yet he desired to live in peace in his beautiful new villa, and he saw that any accommodation with the emperor would involve a resumption of the work at Trent.

70 Protestant cities submit to Charles V after Mühlberg, 1547: a wood relief of 1560

Here accordingly the Council reassembled for a second period (sessions IX to XIV) lasting from May 1551 to April 1552. On this occasion the appearance of a few rather unrepresentative Protestants merely served to reveal the gulf which now separated them from Catholicism, and the documents they offered contained nothing beyond the familiar teachings of the Confession of Augsburg. During this year the Council made little progress except within the important sphere of the eucharist. It clearly asserted the doctrine of trans-substantiation and as clearly condemned the real presence doctrine of Luther, the symbolist doctrine of Zwingli and the medial position adopted by Calvin. The Trent formulae do not, however, enter into scholastic discussions concerning 'substance' and 'accidents'. The sacraments of penance and extreme unction had also been conservatively defined when a new political crisis overtook the council.

The Emperor Charles had defeated the Lutheran princes with the aid of the renegade Lutheran Duke Maurice of Saxony, to whom he transferred the Saxon Electorate. Yet in 1552 this policy rebounded on its author. Demanding more substantial rewards and offended by the emperor's humiliating treatment of his defeated father-in-law Philip of Hesse, Maurice allied with France and drove the luckless emperor southward into Carinthia. The prelates at Trent feared to be seized by the victor and fled in confusion, thus beginning an intermission destined to last a decade. Yet the length of this break was determined less by warfare than by the violently anti-conciliar views of the aged Caraffa, who succeeded to the papal throne as Paul IV in May 1555 and survived for nearly four years. As a Neapolitan he felt a limitless hatred against the Spanish overlords of his native country. As pope he regarded the secular states with contempt and sought to impose on them a theocracy recalling the days of Innocent III. As a former inquisitor he lacked any vestige of tolerance, and thought heretics good enough only for the stake. Disliking conciliarism as at best a source of vain theological chatter, he still maintained the zeal for discipline which in earlier years had led him to collaborate with Contarini, yet he determined to express his zeal in ferocious and highly personal measures. He imprisoned Morone, who had condemned religious persecution and caused Paul to fear that in him a heretic might ascend the papal throne. He sought to strip Reginald Pole of his legatine authority, even though Pole was by now supervising a far from negligible persecution of English heretics.

In Rome itself the pope ruled with an iron hand; he waged a reign of terror against criminals and courtesans, rounded up the multitude of wandering monks and sent two hundred of them to the prisons or the galleys. He sharply reminded the bishops of their duties, forbade dispensations allowing the consecration of bishops below the canonical age, began to check simony and corruption in the Dataria and other curial offices. The chief monument of his zeal lay in the expanding work of the Roman Inquisition, which he supervised personally or through his kindred spirit Ghislieri, the future St Pius V. Here for once he found himself working in harmony with

71 Paul IV's monument, designed by Pirro Ligorio, in the Caraffa Chapel at S. Maria sopra Minerva, Rome

his Spanish foes, and among his many successes the most notable came when he induced the doge to surrender several Venetian heretics to be burned in Rome. Seeing that earlier decrees against heretical books had been largely unavailing, he issued in 1559 the first official Roman Index of prohibited books: an undiscriminating list which included all the works of Erasmus, all the productions of sixty-one named printers and all translations of the Bible into vernacular languages. By his last years the passionate old tyrant was hated even by his own familiars, and the Roman populace took the opportunity of his death to sack the buildings of the Inquisition and burn its records.

119

IX THE LAST PHASE AT TRENT

Following the death of Paul IV the choice of the cardinals fell on the sexagenarian Giovanni Angelo Medici, the son of a Milanese notary unconnected with the great Florentine family. Inevitably, the new pope Pius IV acquired the diminutive title: *Il Medichino*. Having three children to recall his earlier indiscretions, he had not since those days acquired outstanding spiritual gifts. Observers found his personality somewhat unattractive and lacking in dignity; they write of his large red nose, thin beard, rather comic aspect and mincing gait. It seems all the more remarkable that Pius made his brief pontificate one of the most important in the history of the Holy See. Like his predecessors he soon gratified the pleas of his relatives for offices and revenues, yet in the eyes of history he amply atoned by raising to the cardinalate his famous nephew Charles Borromeo, then only twenty-two years of age. Of vastly milder temperament than his predecessor, Pius IV nevertheless proved himself capable of ruthless action against wrongdoers and heretics. Aided by its vices and crimes, he smashed the Caraffa faction and had its leaders, including Cardinal Carlo Caraffa, condemned and executed. While he disliked the powers amassed by the Inquisition he made no effort to dislodge it or to soften its tactics. From Ferrara the inquisitors drove out the heretical Duchess Renée; they assisted Ascanio Colonna—who also received support from the Jesuits—to massacre two thousand members of the Waldensian community in Calabria. And when the duke of Savoy refused to attack the main body of the Waldensians in Piedmont, he received a rebuke from Pope Pius himself.

Meanwhile, the European situation had changed in favour of the Papacy and had begun to offer more favourable prospects for a renewal of the Council. The menacing Empire of Charles V had been divided between his brother Ferdinand and his son Philip. The

72 Pius IV, the astute negotiator who brought Trent to its papalist conclusion; an Italian engraving of 1559

death of Henry II of France had left power in the weak hands of the queen mother, Catherine de Medici, and her young son Francis II. In April 1559 the Treaty of Cateau-Cambrésis had brought peace between the exhausted, almost bankrupt powers. Pius not only saw that a Council was now possible but resolved to make it a success by means of gentle diplomacy. He decided never to repeat the defiant attitudes of Paul IV towards the secular rulers but instead to keep them divided while quietly seeking the co-operation of each.

In this changed world, the Council was summoned back to Trent and began its third period (sessions XV–XXV) in January 1562. As the debates proceeded, it became clear that the orthodox and austere Spaniards would now present the pope and his legates with their severest problems. Though still heavily outnumbered by the Italians, they were organized by Pedro Guerrero, archbishop of Granada, to work as a united and disciplined group. While they resisted all doctrinal novelty, they strove to render the episcopate and the Council independent of the pope, whom they wanted to invest with a primacy of honour rather than one of power. True sons of Spain and allies of her Catholic king, they had every intention of sheltering their national Church from direct papal influence. But the Spaniards were not the only exponents of a nationalist Catholicism. Of the twenty or so French bishops prominent in this third period, most retained the old Gallican spirit and later on this was to be formidably strengthened for a while by the appearance of Charles of Guise, cardinal of Lorraine, scion of a mighty Catholic family then intriguing to dominate France. Needless to add, the lay ambassadors of the great powers remained figures of consequence at every stage.

Pope Pius and his chief legate Morone thus found themselves confronted by various critical groups, which made this phase of the Council much more turbulent than its ultimate success might imply. On the other hand, these groups also conflicted with one another, often failing to amalgamate in the face of the strongest inducements. Again, much of Europe was no longer bringing its problems to be solved in this alleged General Council. England lay firmly under the control of a Protestant government. The German representation remained negligible; so did that from Switzerland, Hungary, Poland, Ireland, Scotland and even Portugal. France apart, the Council represented little more than Mediterranean Europe. The complex patterns of fifteenth-century conciliarism were rapidly simplifying as a new era of Catholic history came to birth.

During the first few months disputes arose concerning a proposed safe-conduct for Protestant delegates to the Council. Apart from the emperor's representatives, few of those at Trent really desired to meet them, yet the legates, anxious to please Ferdinand and throw the onus of refusal upon the Protestants, risked the wrath of King Philip by issuing an invitation. A second controversy of 1562 had a far deeper relevance to the current situation. Was the residence of bishops obligatory by divine right or merely by ecclesiastical law? This seemingly academic question went in fact to the heart of the ecclesiastical system. In raising it the Spaniards were raising the question as to whether episcopal authority derived from God or from the pope. Over this dangerous issue even the legates found themselves divided, and the debates proved so bitter as to be attributed to the direct influence of the devil. After days of coughing, shouting and intermittent uproar the legates managed to get the matter referred

73 St Charles Borromeo (1538–84), founder of seminaries, reliever of the sick and poor in his archdiocese of Milan. This characterization by Daniele Crespi dates from *c.* 1626

to the pope. With more malice than reverence, the French ambassador wrote to a colleague that when divine inspiration was wanted at Trent, it had to be sent in a knapsack from Rome.

During the ensuing deadlock the Council dealt with the demands of the emperor and of the French for the grant of the chalice to the laity. Its denial had been a relatively recent development in the Western Church and was a matter of expediency lacking in theological weight. Here Spanish clericalism stood at one with Roman clericalism, and the counter-pressures of Ferdinand, though strongly backed by the duke of Bavaria, seemed weak compared with those made in earlier years by his brother Charles V. Moreover, in March 1562 came the massacre of Protestants at Vassy and the first of the so-called religious wars in France. The queen mother and the Guises felt the need of papal support, ceased to press for communion in both kinds, and became far less inclined to join with the emperor in coercing Rome. In July the Council decided that it was not of divine obligation to grant the chalice to the laity, that the Church had full authority to regulate the practice, and that the sacrificial Christ is

123

whole and entire under either species of bread and wine. In September the emperor presented his case anew, but Laynez attacked his position with much eloquence, and a majority in effect settled the matter by referring it to the pope.

The other major doctrinal debates of 1562 concerned the sacrificial character of the Mass. When Laynez and Salmeron maintained that the self-oblation of Christ belonged to the Last Supper, the Dominicans (who were destined henceforth to clash so often with Jesuit theology) answered that it took place only upon the Cross. In the end a cautious mediating formula was evolved. The remaining definitions yielded nothing to Protestant criticism: the Mass was decreed a propitiatory sacrifice availing for the quick and the dead; it remained valid even without communicants, and it must be said in the Latin language. On the disciplinary front, the office of quaestor or indulgence-seller was abolished: some thirty-five years too late! To the other ultramontane demands the legates opposed a successful resistance. Certain members continued to press for clerical marriage, others for the reduction of the number of cardinals to twenty-six, yet others for the legal surrender of Church properties to Protestants in actual possession. Needless to add, many desired to see various limitations on the financial and judicial powers of the Curia. Consequently it became the main endeavour of Pius IV to cut off this opposition at its roots by coming to direct agreements with the rulers who had prompted their delegates to make such proposals at Trent.

The last weeks of 1562 and the first of 1563 were nevertheless a parlous time, when the cohesion of the Council and the whole Church seemed on the verge of collapse. The Spaniards were still demanding that episcopal divine right should be recognized. The archbishop of Granada urged that bishops were the brothers, not the sons of the pope, who held his title on the same terms as did any other prelate. The bishop of Segovia argued that in the primitive Church there had been bishops but no Papal Supremacy. Another (echoing Luther's use of *John* xx.23) declared that the keys had been given to the other apostles as well as to St Peter. Laynez attacked these contentions, but he based his case in part upon the Forged Decretals, and he seems to have done more harm than good to the papal

74 Alfonso Salmeron, founder-member of the Society of Jesus; ineffective missionary to Ireland, 1542; colleague of Laynez at Trent

cause by the very eloquence of his attack upon the episcopate. On 13 November there arrived the cardinal of Lorraine accompanied by eighteen French bishops. On the authority of his government he proposed a long list of reforms, including regular preaching and catechizing, clerical marriage, the increased use of the vernacular and the abolition of superstitious observances. Though the curialists and the Spaniards were still contending against each other, the cardinal's programme was so advanced as to offend both, and exchanges of great violence ensued. In one scene Italians and Spaniards denounced each other as 'damned heretics', while in another Laynez declared that the French had been a nation of heretics for the last hundred years. In March 1563 lay factions fought in the streets of Trent, one shouting *Espagna*, the other *Italia*. And as if to exacerbate friends and foes alike, the pope himself made cardinals of a young Gonzaga and a young Medici, aged eighteen and eleven years of age!

Despite such solecisms, Pius found himself able to defy his critics with a growing impunity. Divided against each other, they never joined in common resistance to his legates. In their respective countries, the Imperial and French governments were both faced by formidable Protestant groups: debarred by old secular rivalries from alliance with each other, both needed the friendship of the Papacy. Pius now skilfully selected the able Morone to travel to Innsbruck and win over the emperor, who proved surprisingly apt to be soothed by vague promises of future reform. His ostensible motive was his desire to secure papal recognition of his son Maximilian as successor to the Imperial Crown. In return for the pope's benevolence in this matter Ferdinand undertook to avoid future mention of curial reform, the superiority of Councils over popes, the divine right of episcopacy and other issues obnoxious in Rome. While Maximilian himself reproached his own easy-going parent, Morone returned to Trent in May, reporting triumphantly 'that when people became fully aware of the emperor's friendly dispositions . . . the Council presently changed its aspect, and was much more easily managed.' Though further quarrels lay ahead, the chief danger-point had now been passed. It remained for the Papacy to overcome rearguard resistance, to complete the doctrinal definitions, to set forth some essential disciplinary measures and to dismiss an assembly of which all the participants had become tired.

Among the possible sources of opposition the most formidable was the cardinal of Lorraine, who had been treating almost cordially with the Huguenots at Poissy. Yet his stature in French politics had lately been diminished by the murder of his brother, the duke of Guise. Virtuous, eloquent, well intentioned, brilliantly connected, the owner of a fine personal façade, he lacked the rugged integrity which could have placed him alongside the great figures of his age. More anxious to find new sources of power than to press ruthlessly for reform, the cardinal succumbed to the papal lure and accepted the office of legate apostolic in France. Thenceforward he used his influence to persuade both the queen mother and the Emperor Ferdinand to fall in with the rival programme conceived in Rome. Seeing the emperor still wistfully hoping for clerical marriage and communion in both kinds, the cardinal persuaded him that it would be better to rely upon future direct negotiations with the pope, since the Italians and Spaniards at Trent could never be induced to accept changes so radical.

75 The emphasis placed upon practical charity by reviving Catholicism is reflected in innumerable works of art. 'Clothing the Naked', from *The Works of Mercy* (1525), by Giovanni della Robbia and Santi Buglioni, in the Ospedale del Ceppo, Pistoia

This plea was powerfully reinforced by the Jesuit Peter Canisius, even though both men were seemingly in a position to know that Pius had no intention whatsoever of acceding to such demands. The emperor, much less astute, agreed to the closing of the Council, while the queen mother of France, hoping to secure the pardon of the Church for her peace treaty with the Huguenots, resolved to follow Ferdinand's example rather than to remain in lonely opposition. While at Trent the French joined the Italians, the Spaniards remained the sole group armed with any independence of spirit. Now, however, it was no longer difficult to handle them. Their enthusiasm for practical reform could be accepted whenever it seemed innocuous to curial interests, and whenever it seemed dangerous they could by this stage easily be out-voted. Severe problems would only arise if their distant king were to be roused into dramatic action.

Alongside these dexterous papal manœuvres, the closing months of the Council gave birth to a number of important canons and decrees, some of them vital to the future of the Church. In October, after long and intermittent debates on the sacrament of matrimony, clandestine marriages were invalidated by 133 votes to 59, and ecclesiastical teaching thus brought into line with the civil law of France and Spain. Already in July the debates on holy Orders had ended by decrees enforcing residence on the clergy and providing that a seminary for the training of priests should be erected in every diocese. No proposal of the Council of Trent was to exert more crucial effects than this last. Though slow to be implemented in many dioceses, it meant that the common demand of Colet and Erasmus, of Loyola and Calvin, for better clerical education had at long last been accepted throughout the Church. From this moment all Catholics could maintain a hopeful attitude concerning the chief disciplinary problem: a lower clergy without adequate intellectual and moral formation, incapable of effective preaching and teaching, dubiously equipped to exercise the delicate operations of the confessional. In view of prevalent social attitudes, the Fathers showed much wisdom in their insistence that youths of all classes, poor and rich alike, should be admitted to the new seminaries. While it remains easy to deplore the subsequent tendency of the new colleges towards an ingrowing clericalism, the Church in crisis had no obvious alternative to their creation. The great majority of candidates for the priesthood could not be accommodated by the universities. Moreover, the intellectual and social turmoil of the latter, tempered in only a few places by close collegiate discipline, could not of its very nature provide the intensive professional and spiritual training demanded by the times.

Far from unjustly, opinion at Trent held the temporal governments of Europe in part responsible for the shortcomings and failures of the Church. In August–September 1563 the legates produced some elaborate plans for the 'reform of the princes' and thrust them upon the angry ambassadors present at the Council. No such direct attack could hope to make an impression, if only because some of the most influential prelates were themselves the relatives or officials of princes. Acting for the emperor, the archbishop of Prague demanded the withdrawal of these proposals, and their bold advocates had to be content with some vague decrees prohibiting princely interference in ecclesiastical affairs, calling upon rulers to enforce the decrees of the Council and to respect the rights and properties of the Church.

The remaining legislation was drawn up and rushed through in the dying hours of the Council on 3 and 4 December. The Fathers agreed that purgatory existed, that souls were there aided by the prayers of the faithful and by Masses, that the saints in heaven offer prayers to God for mankind, that it is good and useful to invoke their aid. Further canons imposed reforms on the religious Orders, while a group of enthusiasts alarmed Morone by reviving the old contentions about indulgences. Overnight a cautious decree was prepared reaffirming the use of the latter, while condemning 'all evil gains for the obtaining thereof'. An attempt to forbid all money payments for indulgences narrowly failed, owing in part to the so-called 'crusade Bull' which authorized the Crown of Spain to benefit from indulgence-selling. This matter settled, the final session began at 10 a.m. on 4 December in the cathedral of Trent. It referred to the pope certain tasks left undone: the revision of the Breviary, the Missal and the Index, together with the preparation of an official catechism to compete with those of the Protestants. A further decree confirmed all the Council's previous measures, those passed under Paul III and Julius III as well as those of 1562–3. The Council also prayed Pope Pius to add his confirmation, and this he did in January 1564, appointing in August a special congregation of cardinals to ensure the enforcement of the conciliar legislation. Thus by its last acts the Council implicitly recognized the primacy of the pope, even though at this time the Gallican standpoint alone would have debarred a recognition of papal infallibility in anything like the terms achieved by the Vatican Council of 1870.

It seems no wonder that the Council of Trent ended in an atmosphere of half-incredulous joy and gratitude. 'I myself,' wrote an eyewitness, 'saw many of the most grave prelates weep for joy, and those who had only the day before treated each other as strangers embrace with profound emotion.' And appropriately enough, the assembly broke into a spontaneous burst of cheering for the pope. Seen in the light of history, the Council appears as both creature and creator of the modern Papacy. It ended the long campaign of conciliarism by delivering the Church to a monarchy, one which summoned no other General Council for over three centuries. It led to an apotheosis of papalism more spectacular than the Trent Fathers desired or envisaged. Yet Rome could claim most of the credit for the fact that it attained any conclusive results, that it ended by pulling the Church together rather than tearing it apart. Thanks to the popes and their legates, the fissiparous forces arising from the secular world, from Protestantism and from within Catholicism itself, had been held at bay. So far as concerned the more immediate future, the price paid by the Papacy can hardly be considered high. If Rome abandoned any chance of reconciliation with the Protestant world, that chance had already become minimal. Another condition of success was the granting of a clearer authority to the bishops within their dioceses. Though subordinated to the pope, they now came nearer being masters in their own houses and their authority was less widely eroded by the appeals of their subjects to the Curia. But if this assertion of order and hierarchy touched the pockets of papal officials, it enhanced rather than diminished the real authority of the pope.

In appraising the doctrinal work of the Council, observers have responded all too predictably to their diverse allegiances. The mere historian is hardly equipped to detect or to deny divine inspiration in any of these formularies of faith produced by the sixteenth century. His limited gaze can distinguish a strong strain of Christian idealism at Trent, but it is just as likely to be impressed by the hard bargaining, the clever intrigue, the secular interferences, the elements of compromise. Catholic authors reared in strict clerical traditions tend to accord an inspired inevitability to all its provisions, almost to equate the terms Catholic and Tridentine. In so doing they stand in real danger of becoming involved in circular arguments. So far as continuity is concerned, it should doubtless be acknowledged that Tridentine Catholicism stood far nearer to medieval Catholicism than did any other Church arising from the *mêlée* of the sixteenth century. On the other hand, we do the Fathers of Trent an injustice if we dismiss their doctrinal work as a series of definitions plainly arising from dogmas universally held throughout the medieval centuries. The Council pronounced in fact upon some basic issues concerning which its own members held divergent views, issues upon which a measure of speculative freedom had hitherto existed in the universities and elsewhere.

76 A striking symbol of the Counter Reformation. The Virgin is interceding for Naples, while Luther and Calvin are overthrown, in this fresco by Il Domenichino in Naples Cathedral ▶

Trent was far more than a declaration of war upon Protestant heresies. It was also a victory of some Catholic tendencies over other tendencies which could with much force claim an equal degree of Catholicity. It was a victory for the rising tide of Thomism and a defeat for those Augustinian and biblical-humanist emphases which had helped to stimulate the Protestant Reformation, had become so important for Catholics like Contarini and Seripando and were stubbornly to survive in Jansenism. On the other front, it was a victory over the Occamist and humanist Pelagianism of Erasmus, the *philosophia Christi*, that 'Christianity without tears' which deplored overmuch dogmatic definition. Trent carefully avoided Erasmus while yet travelling as far as possible in the opposite direction from Luther's imputation and his extrinsic righteousness. By placing ecclesiastical tradition on a level with the Bible, it defied the whole Protestant concept of evidence and authority. Still more pointedly, it eschewed Luther's priesthood of all believers, along with the congregationalist implications which arose from that teaching. It was a triumph for the medieval concept of priesthood, an apotheosis of clericalism as well as of papalism. Its educational provisions, unlike those of the Protestant world, centred almost wholly upon the clergy. It did little or nothing to enlarge the responsible roles of laymen and laywomen in the life of the Church. On a somewhat limited front—especially on that occupied by Thomist thinking—it left some room for development in philosophy and theology. Yet on the eve of new scientific discoveries and philosophies, it tended to narrow the sphere of original thought on God, man and the universe. So far as personal religious experience was concerned, it stood on the side of the inquisitors rather than on the side of the great Catholic revivalists and mystics so often in trouble with the Inquisition. Wise after the event, we may now perceive that, in the long run, its clericalism was bound to produce a new wave of anticlericalism. Behind Trent there looms the menacing figure of Voltaire, inflated to superhuman proportions by a process of reaction!

These strictures are easy to make in the context of our own society, which so long ago decided to pay the price for freedom of thought; they will give little offence at a time when Catholics themselves are increasingly critical of Tridentine habits of thought. Yet in its own period-context, Trent corresponded with the demands of many men, who may well have been right in believing that a far larger measure of doctrinal definition had become a crucial necessity for Catholic survival. And even those who judge Trent to have defined too sweepingly, and to have reacted too automatically against anything remotely savouring of Protestantism, may still think that the sheer weight of its intellectual achievement entitles it to a place of honour in Christian history. The canons and decrees remain one of the greatest monuments of committee-thinking in the whole history of religion. Given their general purpose and outlook, their technical perfection and consistency are worthy of the highest admiration. In form and language they are models of clarity and care; they are serviceable documents well abreast of the modern idiom of their day; whatever their debts to scholastic theology, their language is uncluttered by the scholastic habits which had so little relevance to the needs of simple priests and literate laymen. To study them can be a fruitful, almost a moving experience, and this even for readers who normally inhabit very different worlds of thought.

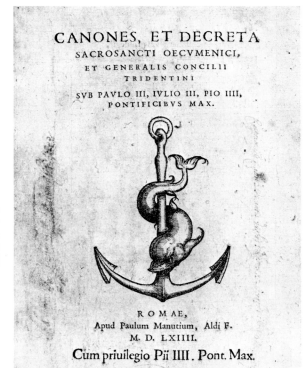

77 Title-page of the *Canons and Decrees* of the Council of Trent (Rome 1564)

X THE REFORMED PAPACY AND THE EUROPEAN POWERS

79 Papal medal commemorating Lepanto (1571)

Endowed with full powers to interpret and implement the Tridentine decrees, the Papacy recovered that commanding position within the Church which it has never since relinquished. Within the half of Europe left to Catholicism it had to fear little save the power of King Philip, who so dangerously interpreted his office as a divine commission. Its confident and authoritarian spirit, incarnated by the grim St Pius V (1566–72), also captured gentler personalities like his successor Gregory XIII (1572–85). Familiar with the wiles of heretics, Pius gave strong support to the Roman Inquisition and stamped out Protestantism in almost all its Italian centres. With equal ardour he persecuted sorcery, while homosexual practices, fashionable in Renaissance Italy, were repeatedly punished by burning. Almost morbidly sensitive to the financial repute of the Curia, Pius abolished annates, indulgence-preaching and other fiscal devices. He halved the expenses of his court, reducing its membership from a thousand to five hundred persons.

His enforcement of clerical residence and monastic discipline was felt not merely within the Papal States but throughout Venice and Naples, the Netherlands and Portugal. Of his many excursions into politics the least debatable and most glorious was his powerful contribution to the victory of Lepanto. Elsewhere, the problems lacked this heroic simplicity. Pius naïvely congratulated the duke of Alva upon the prowess of his 'Council of Blood' in the rebellious Netherlands. In sending troops to help Charles IX of France extirpate heresy, he ordered their commander to take no Huguenot prisoners but slay every one falling into his hands. Having supported the rising of the northern earls against Elizabeth, he issued in 1570 the Bull *Regnans in Excelsis*, deposing her and calling upon her subjects to defy her government.

135

◀ 78 Despite the vast extension of printing, the pulpit remained a powerful weapon. Here the papal nuncio preaches a sermon before Ferdinand I in the Augustinerkirche, Vienna (1560)

Sententia declaratoria contra Elisabeth prætensam Angliæ Reginam, & ei adhærentes Hereticos.

Quæ etiam declarantur absoluti omnes subditi a iuramento fidelitatis & quocunque alio debito

Et deinceps obedientes Anathemate illaqueantur.

P IVS Episcopus Seruus seruorum Dei, Ad futuram rei memoriam.

 EGNANS in excelsis, cui data est omnis in cœlo, & in terra potestas, vnam sanctam Catholicam, & Apostolicam Ecclesiam, extra quam nulla est salus, vni soli in terris videlicet Apostolorum Principi Petro, Petriq. successori Romano Pontifici, in potestatis plenitudine tradidit gubernädam. Hunc unum super omnes gentes, & omnia regna principem constituit, qui euellat, destruat, dissipet, disperdat, plantet, & ædificet: vt fidelem populü mutuæ charitatis nexu constrictum, in unitate spiritus cötineat; saluumq. & incolumem suo exhibeat saluatori. Quo quidem in munere obeundo, nos ad prædictæ Ecclesiæ gubernacula Dei benignitate vocati, nullü laborem intermittimus, omni opera contendentes, ut ipsa unitas, & Catholica religio (quam illius author ad probandam suorum fidem, & correctionem nostram, tantis procellis con flictari permisit) integra conseruetur. Sed impiorum numerus tantum potentia inualuit, ut nullus iam in orbe locus sit relictus, quem illi pessimis doctrinis corrumpere non tentarint; adintente inter cæteros, flagitiorum serua Elisabeth prætensa Angliæ Regina, ad quä

80 Heading of the Bull *Regnans in Excelsis*, by which Pius V deposed Elizabeth I

This revival of the Papacy's highest medieval pretensions came like a bombshell upon the early Elizabethan world, where hitherto there had been virtually no governmental persecution. Here Catholic society was based upon seigneurial households, where rural squires and their dependents observed their religion at home but avoided trouble by minimal attendance at the Anglican churches. Still more disruptive of these easy-going habits was the invasion of the seminary priests trained since 1568 by William Allen at Douai. These emissaries of the continental Counter Reformation were secular clerics, sons of gentle English families whose training during the 1580s took place amid the radical, almost democratic atmosphere of civil war in France. They were dependent on a huge network of communications stretching from Rome and Spain into England, even into turbulent Ireland. After being moved to Rheims, Allen's college was patronized by the Guises and received an annual subsidy from King Philip. Yet once in England its missionaries collaborated uneasily with their hosts, for they insisted upon a total nonconformity towards the Anglican Church established by law.

In our admiration for these heroic men, we should not forget that irreconcilable principles divided the Papacy from the English state. They—and the Jesuits who followed them—were sent by authorities striving to overthrow by any means a government which commanded the loyalty of nearly all Englishmen. One or two found missionary work less congenial than plotting with laymen to murder the queen, and their leaders on the Continent took part in negotiations intended to bring about a foreign invasion and to plunge the country into the abyss which had engulfed France. To such pressure, the Elizabethan government responded from 1581 with a harsh series of penal laws and these, though rather slackly enforced against the laity, had resulted before the end of the reign in the execution as traitors of some 123 missionary priests. Thus at bay, even a more scrupulous government could scarcely have distinguished between the saints and the plotters, between that true martyr Edmund Campion and his less other-worldly friend Robert Parsons. When the former of these two Jesuits faced execution, he was asked whether he renounced the pope, and he replied, 'I am a Catholic.' At this

81 Gregory XIII; a medal of 1572

82 A *Te Deum* in the Sistine Chapel celebrating the Massacre of St Bartholomew; engraving of 1572

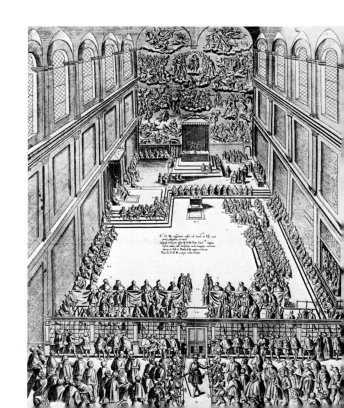

point, a bystander cried, 'In your Catholicism all treason is contained.' Yet the stark dilemma imposed by the Bull of 1570 was rejected by most of the lay Catholics, who desperately wanted to remain loyal Englishmen. A further dichotomy arose when in Elizabeth's last years an acute quarrel developed between an uncompromising group led by Jesuits, and some of the secular priests who now distrusted extremism and sought to gain tolerance from the government in return for their political loyalty. Despite the bigotry of Puritan Parliaments, the English situation now turned against militancy and martyrdom. Among the *émigrés* Benedictine monasticism and mystical studies revived, while in the English court itself there developed a fashionable semi-surreptitious Catholicism.

Meanwhile, when Gregory XIII came to the papal throne there was no thought of relaxing the pressure upon heresy, whether in England or elsewhere. Political and missionary activism continued to be directed from Rome with mounting vigour and confidence. With great liberality the new pope re-endowed all the Jesuit colleges in Rome. Elsewhere he founded over twenty Jesuit establishments, attaching to many of them pontifical seminaries which supplemented the slow and piecemeal efforts of the German and Austrian

83 Henry IV of France

84 A procession of the League
in besieged Paris, 1590;
on such occasions ecclesiastics
handled firearms to the public peril

bishops to re-educate their clergy. Having celebrated the Massacre of St Bartholomew by a *Te Deum*, Gregory helped to consolidate the Catholic League led by the Guises and heavily supported by Spain. In 1579 he sent Nicholas Sanders as papal nuncio to excite rebellion against Elizabeth in Ireland, while in the following year, Campion and Parsons went with his blessing on the English mission.

Under Gregory's successor Sixtus V (1585–90) the Counter-Reformation Papacy attained the height of its influence and prestige. A man of the people, a former vicar general of the Franciscans and a disciple of Pius V, Sixtus had brusque, even boorish manners. He admired only two of his contemporaries: Philip Neri and Queen Elizabeth! His politico-religious activities extended throughout Europe. He helped Stephen Báthory and Sigismund III to advance the Catholic cause in Poland; he induced the duke of Savoy to stage an attack on Geneva; he even imagined himself called by Providence to crush the Ottoman Turks, to conquer Egypt and create a Christian state around the Holy Sepulchre. Much more important, after the assassination of the last Valois king in 1589, he rightly fixed upon the Huguenot heir, Henry IV, as the key to the French situation, and began those overtures which under his successor Clement VIII

(1592–1605) led to Henry's acceptance of Catholicism and entry into Paris. For the Papacy no design could be more important than this pacification of the French wars of religion, for it meant the revival of the only Catholic power which could balance the over-mighty king of Spain.

In Rome itself the rule of Sixtus V crowded a lifetime into five short years. In furtherance of a Tridentine decree of 1546, he made a highly personal attempt at an authentic edition of the Vulgate, and in 1590 set forth the results of his work as not merely official but unalterable. In the event, his embarrassed successor, Clement VIII, had to recover as many copies as possible and to publish (1592) a revised edition with some three thousand corrections. Attributed on the title-page to Sixtus, in order to avoid ridicule, this has commonly and justly been called the Clementine edition. Better success awaited the impatient old pontiff when he undertook tasks more responsive to sheer force of character, in particular when he sought to reorganize the central government of the Church and the Papal States.

Already under Pius IV and Pius V committees of cardinals had been appointed to supervise particular branches of administration. Sixtus now extended and regularized this system by his Bill of 1587, which set up the ministries ever since called Congregations. Some of these he entrusted with secular functions: ensuring the food-supply of Rome, maintaining roads and aqueducts, or examining miscarriages of justice. Others exercised spiritual discipline and included the Congregation of the Inquisition (or Holy Office) and the Congregation of the Council, for the enforcement of the decrees of Trent. This system, greatly expanded in later times, has furnished the chief basis of Roman efficiency, combining centralized power with thoroughness of deliberation. On the principle *divide et impera*, it diminished the power of the Sacred College as compared with that of the popes. There can be few states in history which have undergone so swiftly any comparable degree of administrative rationalization. Further central reforms occurred at various stages of the Counter-Reformation period. In the previous year Sixtus fixed the number of cardinals at seventy and laid down

85 This bronze bust of Sixtus V from Treia Cathedral conveys his singular force of character

86 Clement VIII (1592–1605) recognized Henry IV, issued the definitive edition of the Vulgate and placed British Catholics in the charge of archpriests

precise qualifications for the office. For some time to come, these latter rules were often ignored, while until quite recent times this stipulation that cardinals should be chosen from the best men of every Christian country was never suffered to disturb the overwhelming majority of Italians in the Sacred College. As for the elaborate procedures calculated to avoid intrigue and collusion at papal elections, these were imposed by the legally trained Gregory XV as late as 1621–2.

We modern lovers of the city of Rome see the supreme achievement of Sixtus V in that planned metropolis which has ever since constituted a major missionary force in its own right. Here Sixtus found a series of fragmentary developments devised by his predecessors. Aided by Domenico Fontana, he drew these schemes together into one master-plan, and connected the seven great pilgrimage churches by a pattern of roads which triumphantly crossed every hill and valley. For centuries the healthy hill-areas within the Aurelian Walls had been almost inaccessible and uninhabited. Now the new roads speedily attracted buildings, and people returning to Rome after a few years' absence declared they could scarcely recognize it as the city they had left. With an unerring

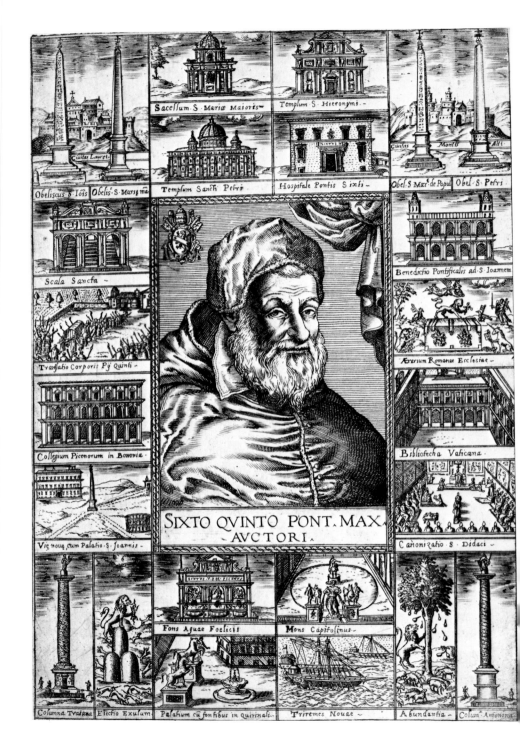

Sacellum S. Mariæ Maioris

Templum S. Hieronymi

Obeliscus S. Ioïs | Obelis S. Mariæ ma

Civitas Lauret.

Templum Sancti Petri

Hospitale Pontis Sixti

Civitas | Montis | Alti

Obel. S. Mariæ de Populi | Obel. S. Petri

Scala Sancta

Translatio Corporis Pÿ Quinti

Collegium Picenorum in Bononia

Vis noua cum Palatio S. Joannis

Benedictio Pontificalis ad. S. Ioannem

Ærarium Romanæ Ecclesiae

Bibliotheca Vaticana

Canonizatio S. Didaci

SIXTO QVINTO PONT. MAX.
AVCTORI.

Columna Traiana | Electio Exulum

Fons Aquae Foelicis

Palatium cu fontibus in Quirinali

Mons Capitolinus

Triremes Nouae

Abundantia

Colum. Antonina

sense of spatial possibilities the pope placed his famous obelisks on the spots which developed into the noble squares of later years. The city, hitherto unable to match the great civic cores of Venice, Florence and Siena, now developed a whole complex of them. So prepared by Sixtus, she awaited Bernini and his contemporaries, who in the next generation completed the scheme by ranges of superb public buildings.

This greatest practical organizer ever to occupy the papal throne was no megalomaniac but a true exponent of urban renewal, conceived in its social as well as in its monumental objectives. Purchasing springs of fresh water near Palestrina, he introduced the Aqua Felice through seven miles of tunnel and seven miles of arched aqueduct, thus bringing water to the highest places in the city's hills. Near its point of entry the formidable Moses fountain is intended as a reminder that these areas had lain desiccated since the fall of the Empire. Near by in the Piazza delle Terme the pope installed a large public washing-place for the women of Rome, while the fountain of Trevi he originally provided as a basin for the rinsing of wool. Sixtus in fact strove to restore the woollen and silk industries of the city, and had he lived a year longer he would have transformed the Colosseum into a colony of spinners, who would have lived in the upper stories and had their workshops in the former arena. This resurgence of Rome as a living city of the people should not be linked, as it often is, with the embellishment of the Vatican by the Renaissance popes. It has a clearly different significance and justly represents an autocracy endued with a larger spirit. Likewise, the revival of Rome as a Christian city belongs in large part to the second half of the sixteenth century. It is chiefly associated with Philip Neri, that most amiable of her citizens, most human of her saints, whose work we shall shortly describe.

More than any other, St Philip brought to the Catholic Reformation the themes of Christian affection and joy. Yet these themes even he would have found hard to demonstrate upon the frontiers of Catholic Europe. Here the leadership inevitably fell to harder spirits, more purposeful organizers, among whom St Peter Canisius stood supreme. A bare chronicle of his immense journeys and

◀ 87 Portrait of Sixtus V, showing the achievements of his pontificate

solid achievements might suggest the spiritual martinet, the man of iron. Yet alongside his unwavering resolution, his toughness, stability and patience, the great Jesuit possessed no small fund of humanity. It is true that he cannot be made a hero of liberal or ecumenical Catholicism. At the Colloquy with the Protestants in 1557, he pronounced the whole affair pointless, and he made merciless use of the internal quarrels between the followers of Melanchthon and the strict Lutherans under Flacius Illyricus. Like most Jesuits of his day, he had the overwhelming will to win; like most Christians of his day, he did not reject the claims of the civil power to persecute and punish heretics. Nevertheless, such were not his chosen weapons, and his successes were gained far less through police action than through organizing ability, self-dedication and the deployment of persuasive arguments. He sought to break away from the mutual bludgeoning of Eck and Luther; he insisted on courtesy and suavity and so shone alongside the abusive Flacius. A countryman of Erasmus who adopted all the German-speaking peoples, Canisius rose supreme above narrow nationalisms. In high credit with the Emperor Ferdinand I, he became the best interpreter of the Teutons to the dignitaries of Rome, whose cultured contempt for non-Italians had hitherto so gravely injured the unity of the Church. Despite the excellence of his famous Catechism, he was no literary genius. And unless genius be rightly defined as an infinite capacity for taking pains, he was scarcely even a religious genius. His biographer Fr Brodrick has used the term 'sublime mediocrity' to characterize his work. Maintaining a vivid devotion to the person of Christ, he was no high mystic but rather addicted to the modest popular cults, the Rosary and the Hours of the Virgin. Perhaps his very lack of imagination helped to inoculate him throughout his exhaustive studies of heresy against any danger of seeing a Protestant viewpoint. He could boast little historical or critical sense; his writings on the saints do not make him a fore-runner of the learned Bollandists, for historical truth interested him far less than the devotional use of his themes. Men of this stamp believed history to be wholly on their side; with little effort they seem to have rejected the possibility that during the last ten centuries

88 St Peter Canisius (1521–97), most successful of the Jesuit agents of reconquest in Europe

the Church might have embarked upon some sub-Christian courses. But alongside his untroubled, highly functional intelligence Peter Canisius had the advantage of a heartfelt sympathy with the popular religion; he ended by becoming a saint for ordinary, prosaic men, especially for those unfortunate enough to be born outside Renaissance Italy.

In 1566 Pius V wrote to the bishop of Münster, 'we learn that the chief cause of such gross heresy in Germany is the wicked, indecent and disgraceful conduct of the clergy.' The reality of the Jesuit achievement in central Europe can only be assessed by reference to the small progress made there by the Catholic Reformation during its earlier decades. Our previous accounts of religious revival apply little enough to these areas. A host of Catholic observers extending into the 1580s – Commendone, Staphylus, Nunguarda, Gropper, Minutio Minacci – are singularly agreed concerning the prevalence of gross ignorance and concubinage among the parish clergy. Almost equally do they dwell on the alarming secularism of the cathedral chapters in places like Regensburg, Würzburg and Augsburg, for long after the mid-century the canons were reputed to be chiefly concerned with horses,

145

dogs and women. Even the exalted ecclesiastics who understood the need for reform and who backed the Jesuits were slow to emulate Jesuit dedication and single-mindedness. A letter of Canisius to the free-spending Cardinal Truchsess insists courteously but firmly that the prelate's finances cannot extend to support luxuries like fine choirs, and at the same time to promote Jesuit enterprises.

The great work of Canisius began as early as 1549 when, returning to Germany along with Le Jay and Salmeron, he began to preach at Ingolstadt under the patronage of the duke of Bavaria. Three years later he transferred his headquarters to Vienna and found Austrian Catholicism still struggling for existence not only against Lutheran missionaries and magnates but also against a varied array of sectarians. During the subsequent years, often working against extreme financial embarrassment, he founded Jesuit university colleges at Ingolstadt, Cologne, Nymegen, Prague and Innsbruck. Alongside these he established another series of colleges for boys, thus promoting Catholic influence among leading families while at the same time securing recruits of quality for the priesthood. From 1563 he even accepted the management of the small university at Dillingen, which in the event attained but little success. Active among the present and future leaders of society, he was plagued by acrid disputes between his own followers concerning the *Contractus Germanicus*, a form of investment at five per cent. On this antiquated problem of business ethics, pious lenders could elicit no unanimous guidance from the Jesuits. Somehow Canisius also found time and energy to undertake popular evangelism. During 1561–2 he spent some eighteen months in Augsburg, with its strong Protestant faction: during that period he is recorded as preaching between 200 and 225 sermons in the cathedral. Gradually he trained a host of helpers, and when he left central Europe after thirty years of heroic toil no less than 1100 Jesuits were at work in the German lands.

With the figures of Peter Canisius and Sixtus V we enter a frontier-world in which the secular and the religious are hopelessly blurred. In that age nobody expected men of religion to reject alliances offered by the secular states. As for the popes, they were themselves secular rulers and exposed to manifold perils in one of the cockpits of Europe. They were called to reconcile mundane with spiritual responsibilities, regional with universal functions. This was a desperate situation thrust upon them by history, one which simply did not admit of ideal solutions, yet one in which personal virtues now began to pay better worldly dividends than Machiavelli would have supposed possible when he wrote his famous passage on the inevitable ruin awaiting 'unarmed prophets'.

In the Holy Roman Empire convulsed by Luther, a league of Catholic rulers was bound to emerge as soon as the Habsburg emperor condemned the arch-heretic and started looking for allies. Such a league already existed when at Regensburg in June 1524 the Archduke Ferdinand, the Bavarian dukes and twelve prince-bishops agreed in the presence of the papal nuncio Campeggio to execute the Edict of Worms against Luther, to fight his heresy and to press for reforms of discipline and doctrine within the Church. Yet no responsible German prince on either side wanted to see the Empire ruined by open war, and even the Catholic rulers came to realize that a Habsburg despotism might well spring from a successful anti-Protestant crusade. The kings of France saw this with equal clarity; hence they swallowed their Catholicism to support the Lutheran princes and their Christianity to support the Ottoman Turks. When war at last erupted in 1547, the emperor wisely refused to pose as a religious crusader, and after many military disappointments he had by 1555 to accept the Peace of Augsburg, which allowed each prince to dictate the religion of his subjects and to expel nonconformists.

The long-ensuing truce in central Europe favoured the work of Canisius, but elsewhere the Counter Reformation was soon caught up in further political upheavals, especially in the Netherlands revolt and in the French wars of religion. Both these cataclysms were clearly linked with Reformation and Counter Reformation, yet their religious components are often overestimated. The latter seems essentially a struggle for power between the Valois, the Guises, the Bourbons and other great Houses of France. Every region had groups and feuds related to the main struggle; local interests and family traditions often determined confessional and hence military allegiances, while a range of social and economic pressures prolonged the struggle from decade to decade. Soldiering was a way of life and a means of livelihood for the swarming gentry of France, hard hit as they were by monetary inflation and by the cessation of the Italian wars. Moreover, many sincere French Catholics were guiltless of fanaticism. The distinguished group of *politiques* never ceased to demand religious tolerance and to call for the subordination of confessional hatreds to the claims of a paternal monarchy. Yet as time passed, religion did tend to rally the factions under national banners. The rise of bourgeois leaders among the Huguenots supplied a new element of fervour; so, on the other side, did the rise of the Guises and the Catholic League. When in 1589 Henry of Navarre, still a Huguenot, succeeded the last of the Valois and besieged Catholic Paris, a genuine war of religion seemed at hand. The starving, hysterical community was inflamed by radical· pamphleteering and turgid sermons, even by parades of monks, who were apt to injure bystanders through their inexpert attempts to handle firearms. Yet in July 1593 the king suddenly lowered the dispute to the secular plane by announcing his conversion to Catholicism.

Parallel considerations suggest a cautious attitude to the religious elements in the struggle between Philip and the Netherlands. This episode had some military and ideological links with the French wars, yet in essence it was the birth of a nation, the effort of a group of hitherto locally minded towns and provinces to coalesce against a foreign overlord. But the provocations were numerous. The first opposition was largely aroused by Philip's threat to the secular interests of the nobility; its extension to the merchant classes and the people sprang as much from the horrors of Spanish taxation as from those of the Spanish Inquisition. Certainly that strange outcome in the division of the northern from the southern Netherlands arose from geographical and strategic factors. It cannot be attributed to cultural divisions or to any prior religious conquest of the north by Calvinism, which in fact had most of its earlier centres in the southern cities. And while Philip announced that he was merely punishing secular rebels, William the Silent was far less a hero of the Reformation than a cool aristocrat calling upon the Netherlands to place the patriot cause before their religious emotions. On the other side, however, it must be acknowledged that convinced Calvinists did tend to attain the leadership of many Dutch towns and cities, even of those where Catholics and religious temporizers greatly out-numbered them. This Calvinist leadership doubtless helped to give a cutting edge to the whole revolt, even though it failed to retain a monopoly of power in the seven provinces which broke free to become the Dutch Republic. From a positive Catholic viewpoint, the important result was that the other ten provinces were kept within the fold. The reconciling Jesuits flocked in behind the victorious forces of the duke of Parma. Flanders and Brabant, long a major focus of European civilization and hitherto having close cultural affinities with Holland, now became a major outpost of Catholicism in northern Europe.

Admitting the complexity of the links between resurgent Cathol-icism and these political struggles, can we rightly think of a league of Counter-Reformation powers striving in concert for Tridentine orthodoxy, for effective papal headship of a united Christendom? The credibility of this idea must stand or fall on the record of the Church's alleged champion-in-chief: Philip II of Spain. Yet by any standards this record must be pronounced unimpressive. So far from establishing a steady crusading alliance with Rome, Philip was in constant and often bitter conflict with the popes over matters of foreign policy and ecclesiastical jurisdiction. A subject of Philip could no more appeal to Rome than could a subject of Queen Elizabeth. The king continued to enjoy as a permanent tax the subsidy granted by earlier popes to finance the crusade; he continued also to appoint to every bishopric and to most other wealthy benefices in Spain. When after a whole year's hesitation he agreed to publicize the decrees of Trent, it was only with the proviso that his control over the Spanish clergy should remain untouched. For their part, the latter could be relied upon in any dispute with Rome to back the king, who had appointed them. In the classic dispute over

89 'Simplicity of form, severity in the whole, nobility without arrogance, majesty without ostentation'—Philip's instructions to Herrera, who finished the Escorial in 1584

Carranza, Philip not only allowed his Inquisition to level monstrous charges of Lutheranism against the archbishop; he maintained the attack in the face of all papal protests for a period of some sixteen years. And at no stage did he fail to extract every advantage from his position in Naples and from the pope's need for his naval support in the Mediterranean.

All things considered, the constant rifts between the Escorial and the Vatican cannot be dismissed as the bickering of allies with a fundamental unity of purpose, for they had become integral to the structure of Catholic Christendom. In that narrowed world Rome had to work for a balance of Catholic powers; she had every reason

90 Unlike the Baroque flatterers of Louis XIV, El Greco kept the ruler in his place; detail from *The Dream of Philip II*

to fear a Spanish hegemony and to long for the revival of war-torn France. That Philip burned heretics was far less important to Rome than that he strove with prolonged success to enfeeble France. Whereas the Renaissance popes had tended to remain parochial Italians, their post-Tridentine successors thought and planned on a broad, supranational scale. Between their thinking and Philip's harsh Spanish nationalism a profound gulf existed. The attitudes of Philip and his subjects illustrate the innocence with which men of that century identified the interests of elect nations with the divine purpose. Thinking of chosen peoples as opposed to inferior breeds, it may be worth remembering that Old Testament studies flourished as much in racialist Spain as in any Protestant country. And in complete fairness one should also recall that Renaissance Italians had claimed for themselves a similar distinction without either biblical or crusading inspirations; they merely applied to all other nations the old pagan word *barbari*!

The saga of the would-be Catholic champions has its next striking figure in the Emperor Ferdinand II (reigned 1619–37) who in earlier life had distinguished himself as a persecuting ruler of Styria. The cautious attitudes prescribed in 1555 at Augsburg had already begun to break down under the Jesuit-educated Rudolph II (reigned 1576–1612), but no sequel could have been more disastrous than the succession of Ferdinand, for he combined a solemn belief in the divine mission of the Habsburgs with a devout mind and a large fund of political tenacity. He began the Thirty Years War with powerful aid from Bavaria. Having overthrown the elector palatine in Bohemia, having driven Christian IV into the Danish islands and stationed an army on the Baltic, he issued the Edict of Restitution (1629), aimed at recovering all the enormous German lands lost to the Church since 1552. This ambitious attempt to achieve a territorial Counter Reformation Ferdinand made through Wallenstein, a new-style *condottiere* who literally believed in his own star and who, like Oliver Cromwell, sought to 'cast the Kingdom old into another mould'. Such a degree of radicalism could not long harmonize with the emperor's dynasticism. The consequent murder of the embarrassing Wallenstein (1634) had, however, been preceded by the formidable Swedish invasion of the Empire, and it was followed by the involvement of France under Richelieu and Mazarin. The spectacle of Gustavus Adolphus rolling back Catholicism from northern Germany bids us recall the fact that in 1578 Jesuits in disguise had reconverted his predecessor John III of Sweden, but had been forbidden by Rome to offer that country communion in both kinds, clerical marriage and the vernacular Mass. Two years later, having failed to make more than a handful of converts, they had been hunted out, missing a slender chance to alter the whole tide of European history. Thanks to Lutheran Sweden, at the Peace of Westphalia (1648) the results of the Imperial Counter Reformation were hence relatively modest; it had further consolidated the hold of Catholicism upon the Habsburg lands, upon Bavaria and the prince-bishoprics. It had brutally imposed Catholicism upon Bohemia. One might argue that Ferdinand had accomplished less than Canisius at an incomparably greater cost.

So far as concerns the internal policies of the Catholic rulers, some historians have found it all too easy to generalize concerning their intolerant views and harsh persecutions. Yet in that age the two most notable experiments in governmental toleration both occurred in countries where Catholicism predominated: France and Poland. These experiments were admittedly of limited duration, but until the middle of the seventeenth century little difference seems observable in this matter of toleration between the Catholic and the Protestant states. From that period onwards, it is true, rationalist, utilitarian and sectarian ideas began to gain the upper hand in most Protestant states, where intolerant ecclesiastics were losing their grip. On the other hand, the absolutist Catholic rulers, even the less religious among them, continued to regard heresy as not merely divisive but as an affront to the majesty of the prince. Whereas Richelieu had been content to clip the political and military wings of the Huguenots, Louis XIV embarked on an insensate persecution, justifiable neither by political dangers nor by any deeply-felt desire to save souls. By now France had much solid piety and many good parish priests, but her great saints had all gone to their reward. At Versailles the glorious periods of Bossuet reverberated in a pious vacuum; in a dull court Madame de Maintenon presided over the king's personal salvation, while in the royal chapel the courtiers sat with their backs to the altar so as to face the king. Only a shade more excusably in our eyes, some of the German and Austrian prince-bishops were still organizing mass-expulsions of their heretical subjects in the eighteenth century.

In the age of the Counter Reformation itself there existed among Catholic political thinkers many degrees of liberalism and illiberalism. This is likewise true of state policies, even in those countries where Catholicism triumphed. In Poland it happened to find a great early leader in Cardinal Hosius (d. 1579), who combined a native's grasp of local conditions with the closest possible contact with Rome. The Polish Counter Reformation adapted itself with no little success to the spirit and needs of that people. The case of Bohemia stands in unhappy contrast. There the nation had long ago found its identity in the Hussite revolution, and though the latter had shown marked fissiparous tendencies, its chief parties had deep roots in Czech society, roots which had not been weakened by the coming of the Protestant Reformation. When in 1618 the nobility revolted in the face of Ferdinand's open threats to their liberties and churches, they unwisely decided to offer the Bohemian crown to the incapable elector palatine. But they had one far more fatal gap in their armoury. A peasantry now reduced to serfdom had lost the patriotic fervour of the Hussite wars. Ferdinand's victory at the White Mountain (1620) was followed by seven years of reprisals. Some three-quarters of the land (excluding that of king and Church) was transferred to the emperor's agents and mercenaries, while a new, absolutist constitution allowed only the empty shell of national independence.

More violent still was the ecclesiastical reaction supervised by the papal nuncio Giovanni Caraffa. The Bohemian pastors were expelled, all Protestant schools closed, the famous Charles University and other places of higher education put into the hands of the Jesuits. Fines and sentences of imprisonment brought the towns to heel, at least outwardly. Some thirty-six thousand families—perhaps a quarter of the landowners and urban population—emigrated to avoid accepting Catholicism, though the serfs were not offered that option. Meanwhile, Upper Austria was purged of heresy by similar measures. The persecution of these years rivalled any hitherto undertaken by the Habsburgs, except perhaps their actions in Spain against the *moriscos*. Bearing heavily upon both Protestant and Catholic Reformations were these inheritances which disposed of whole peoples. The English in Ireland and the Spaniards in the Netherlands are at least worthy to be included in the same category, though both stood on stronger legal grounds than did Ferdinand in the ancient kingdom of Bohemia. Neither came so near to destroying the continuity of a nation.

91 Ferdinand II
(Emperor 1619–37),
who sought to re-create
by force a Catholic
Habsburg Empire

Such, however, were not the saddest involvements of European Christianity in episodes of secular oppression. More detestable still were some of the developments outside Europe, wherein religion (whether Catholic or Protestant) was twisted to provide a rationale for depriving non-Europeans of human rights. No more flagrant perversions of the Christian Gospel could be imagined, and there were at least a few men of the Counter Reformation who swiftly recognized their enormity. No religious action was more truly enlightened or more pertinacious than the campaign of Bishop Las Casas (d. 1566) to secure humane treatment for the Indian populations of Central and South America. Some of the abuses he attributed to the Spanish colonists in his *Destruction of the Indies* (1552) seem

155

even to have exceeded the ugly truth. And Las Casas himself believed that the importation of Negro slaves could be justified! Today we tend to pay more attention to the demographers than to the hagiographers. In 1519, when Cortés landed in Mexico, the native population seems to have numbered some 25 millions. As early as 1548 about 18½ millions had vanished, and by 1575 only 2 millions survived. Throughout this appalling episode, it is true that Western diseases had been at work alongside the forced labour of the mine and the *encomienda*. If Spain, long involved in warfare against the infidel, could hardly have made an ideal colonizing power, it is also to be admitted that English, Portuguese and Dutch settlers were soon to prove themselves just as capable of unfeeling greed and hypocrisy.

No religion has ever subdued whole nations to exalted ethical convictions and conduct: only to a limited extent should we saddle a religion with the sins of its nominal adherents. Yet the early history of colonization does suggest that Europe was exporting a great deal of its narrow racialism, its self-deceptions, its least Christian dregs, as well as a little of its Christian sanctity. Amid this process the Counter Reformation played, or at least permitted, some ambivalent roles. The Jesuits, identified in some colonial backgrounds with persecution, ended by making in seventeenth-century Paraguay the first and most moving attempt to create a paternalist Utopia, insulated from the wicked world.

92 Plate from a German translation (1599) of Las Casas, *Destruction of the Indies*

XI THE FLOWERING OF THE
CATHOLIC REFORMATION

Born a Florentine, inheriting the free and independent spirit of his native city, perhaps not immune from the heritage of Savonarola, Philip Neri (1515–95) sought a middle course between the uncouth, self-appointed prophets who so often called Rome to repentance, and the disciplinarians like Pius V or the early Jesuits. A natural humorist, outwardly a mild eccentric, he hated no sin more than that of stuffy and arrogant pietism. Though alarmed by visionaries—and especially by females of the species—he nevertheless wielded strange psychiatric powers of his own. Able to soothe afflicted minds, he strove to control and conceal his own unsought abstractions and ecstasies. This did not make him the exponent of any rigid method. He felt that sanctity consisted in the development of each man's unique gifts, that it should not be conceived in uniform patterns or allowed to distort individual personality. In 1548 he began to form a brotherhood devoted to prayer and discussion, yet also to aiding the poor and the pilgrims who thronged the city streets. His prayer-meetings, graced by the music of his friend Palestrina, ultimately gave birth to the term *oratorio*. By 1564 he had formed the Congregation of the Oratory and directed it increasingly to the rehabilitation of the priesthood in the service of lay people. His work soon attracted the notice of the great, and in a surprisingly choleric letter he upbraids Archbishop Charles Borromeo for attempting to draw off all his best men to Milan. Though Philip had been largely self-educated, his Order attracted scholars and intellectuals, the most famous of later years being Caesar Baronius (d. 1607), the historian whose *Annales Ecclesiastici* attacked the Lutheran version of Christian history embodied in the *Magdeburg Centuries.*

St Philip remained the most affectionate, the least polemical of men. Almost alone among his contemporaries, he treated the Jews

94 S. Maria in Vallicella,
assigned to Neri
for his Oratorians
and rebuilt 1580–1605;
a papal medal of 1575

93 A Baroque impression (1647)
of St Philip Neri
by Guercino

of Rome not only with personal gentleness but with a sincere respect for their principles and their faith. But he would not have been a man of his age had he not quietly converted a few of them as opportunities arose! Backed by the fabulously rich Cardinal Cesi, he began rebuilding the church of S. Maria in Vallicella, assigned to him by Gregory XIII. In the same year (1575) he inspired all Rome to new feats of lodging and catering on behalf of the pilgrims to the Jubilee. Meanwhile, the houses of Oratorians had begun to multiply throughout Italy and Europe. Curiously un-Roman in their lack of a central organization, they nevertheless survived many perils. Philip's ideals ultimately inspired Pierre de Bérulle to found the French Oratory in 1611, and despite some propensities toward Jansenism, it produced a succession of saints, scholars and seminary-teachers, who exerted marked influences upon other founders like St Vincent de Paul and more generally upon both educated and popular religion in France. The British parallel came only in the last century, when Cardinal Newman introduced the Oratorians to an important role in British Catholicism.

A very different idiom marks the Spanish Carmelites, St Teresa of Àvila (1515–82) and St John of the Cross (1542–91). These two august and original personalities should not be tied too closely to any tradition. There did indeed exist a 'Spanish Carmelite' school containing several lesser luminaries, yet among Teresa's own spiritual guides were three Jesuits, three Dominicans, a Franciscan and two secular priests. Only in her later years was she concerned with the Carmelites Jerónimo Gracián and St John, at once her disciples and her counsellors. As for John's mystical theology, it looks most closely related to older foreign traditions, to the work of Tauler, which he probably knew, and to *The Cloud of Unknowing*, which he surely cannot have read. Together he and Teresa carried the contemplative approach to its zenith; in both, experience is so obviously first hand as to discourage the most hardened academic source-hunter. It can be shown, for example, that Teresa knew a good deal about Augustine, Jerome, Gregory, the *Imitation* and Ludolph of Saxony's popular *Life of Christ*, yet from these and even from the recent Spanish mystical authors she appears to have borrowed little save a few technical terms and illustrations. At one point of her autobiography she describes her occasional intuitions of a divine presence, and then she blandly adds, 'This was no kind of vision; I believe it is called *mystical theology*.'

95 St Teresa,
the contemporary portrait
(1576) by Fray Juan
de la Miseria

A similar independence is clear in St John, but alongside it there appears a profound and searching reference of the spiritual life to biblical criteria. 'If we are guided by divine Scripture,' he remarks, 'we shall not be able to err, for he who speaks in it is the Holy Ghost.' Less the spontaneous, instinctive explorer than Teresa, he was not merely the great poet but the great theologian of mysticism. In Teresa there are elements which would be dismissed by any modern reader as superstitions of her age, yet she too is not unaware of the dangers of auto-suggestion. In their caution, in the robust good sense they apply to deep and harrowing experiences, they are both among the highest aristocracy of the contemplative tradition. Ever under suspicion as *Alumbrados* or Quietists, they took pains to show their innocence of such charges. Firm in the doctrine that human devotions are powerless without divine grace, they nevertheless insist that the soul never attains a passivity which enables it to renounce responsibility or claim to be a mere divine instrument. As for visions, locutions, raptures and trances, Teresa knew that these could as readily come from the devil as from God; on her deathbed she gave thanks that she was a daughter of the Church, beside which no vision could claim significance. She believed moreover that a contemplative must submit to the guidance of learned men, even if these were not the recipients of mystical experience. While far from subservient in practical matters, she obeyed her confessor in preference to the supposed commands of Christ, seen in a vision. As for St John, he has a scorn for the sensational which would do credit to a modern rationalist. Both of them tried to chart in some detail the stages of progress and the obstacles experienced by a contemplative soul, from the time it uses elementary discursive prayer to its possible—but on this earth rarely attained— union with the divine. In his remarkable work *The Crucible of Love*, Dr E. W. T. Dicken has compared their respective schemes in new and brilliant detail; despite some divergences, the two patterns remain broadly similar.

Few students of the great mystics can avoid asking themselves the question: what, if any, non-subjective forces underlie these mutually corroborated stories? In this regard the literature of mysticism seems to the present writer fascinating but inconclusive; nor has modern psychiatry mastered all the data. Yet that the higher states bestowed upon their subjects astonishing resources of mental power will hardly be disputed. In December 1577 the unreformed Carmelites kidnapped St John, imprisoned him at Ávila, removed him to Toledo, kept him in a tiny dungeon on bread, water and salt fish, flogged him often and allowed him no change of clothing, so that the clotted blood made his habit stick to his skin. At the same time they sought with great mental cruelty to assure him that all his labours had been in vain. But amid this torment of mind and body he wrote the first thirty stanzas of the *Spiritual Canticle*.

So many of the great figures of the Spanish Church were persecuted on suspicion of heresy: not only these Discalced Carmelites but Luis de Granada, Bartolomé Carranza, Luis de Leon, Juan de Ávila (the 'Apostle of Andalusia'). If we readily see Spain as the land of mystics, we must also acknowledge the violence of the clerical and official forces opposed not only to contemplation but to the monastic reforms which sprang from its demands. For Teresa and John, the practical tasks came as no mere tidy afterthought. In the last resort their spiritual values depended on the survival of genuine monasticism. While Teresa often played the scolding perfectionist, there was nothing imaginary about the low state of the religious houses which she sought to improve: many were elegant hostels for gossiping women, with the occasional case of hysteria passing for sanctity. Her viewpoint upon the Counter Reformation is well expressed in her saying, 'No wonder the Church is as it is, when the religious live as they do.' This remark was perfectly realistic in that setting, where monastic affairs were woven into the texture of society: the whole town of Ávila, for example, was convulsed by the feuds arising over problems of monastic reform. Today the guidance and extension of an Order of nuns may seem to pale into insignificance beside the personal influences of Teresa's writings. But she herself would have regarded with alarm this cult of personality. That she was condemned to journey painfully many months of every year through cold and heat across the iron landscapes of Castile seemed no mere distraction from the consolations

96 The supreme development of Mannerism and a great monument of Catholic spirituality: El Greco's *Burial of Count Orgaz*

97 Fray Luis de Leon, from a drawing published 1599

and ardours of the interior life. She was not among those many unprivileged spirits of her day, who suffered such disciplines and did so many good deeds out of pride, taking the ascetic life as a mask to cover their emptiness rather than as a means to love God.

The ineffable character of mystical experience has seldom retarded its attempts to find literary expression. The many devotional handbooks, the natural, tumultuous prose of St Teresa and the soaring verses of St John—these by no means exhaust the genres of mystical literature. Further dimensions appear in the works of Fray Luis de Leon (*c.* 1528–91), the renowned Augustinian who from 1561 occupied theological chairs at Salamanca. Soon after that date he began to fall foul of various enemies in the university and the Inquisition. His subsequent troubles sprang in part from his blistering scorn towards pedants, in part from his refusal as a humanist to bow before the golden calf of the Vulgate text. Perhaps they arose most of all from his friendships with Benito Arias Montano and other teachers of Hebrew, who faced charges of issuing Jewish propaganda or favouring rabbinical interpretations of the Bible. And Fray Luis, be it remembered, had also been imprudent enough to translate the Song of Solomon into Spanish for the benefit of a nun!

163

After four years of imprisonment and long inquiries, the local committee of the Inquisition recommended that torture be applied to him, adding that in view of his poor health 'a moderate amount of agony' should suffice to extract the truth. But in December 1576 a higher authority forestalled the experiment by ordering his release. He returned in triumph to the university, resuming his course of lectures with the words, 'As I was saying yesterday . . .'. Though further vain attempts were made to depose him from his chair, his Order elected him provincial of Castile a few days before his death.

The career and writings of Luis de Leon display a versatility and a boldness which derive more from the Italian Renaissance than from the constricted fervours of the Castilian Counter Reformation. A warm admirer of the mystics, he wrote a famous life of St Teresa, whom he never met but admirably understood. On the other hand, as humanist, philosopher and theologian he attained a commanding stature among the intellectuals of his day. Above all, he wrote that small group of original lyrics upon which his modern fame chiefly depends. Most of them are rare masterpieces attaining a gracious fusion of classical with mystical themes and evincing intuitive powers which to an English reader recall Vaughan or even Wordsworth. If one felt stifled by the Spanish setting, or regarded the Carmelites as too remote from our mundane lives, it would still be a pity to miss the *Noche Serena*, the *Morada del Cielo*, or the ode to the organist Salinas. Luis and his younger contemporary El Greco (1541–1614) can scarcely be dubbed 'typical figures' of the Spanish Counter Reformation. Yet to understand with love at least some of its facets, one should know well half a dozen poems by Luis, and should visit the little church of Santo Tomé in Toledo, where the 'Burial of Count Orgaz' transcends the painter's normal achievement. In both poetry and painting, human dignity manages to coexist with ecclesiastical governance, while both affirm that the meaning of life lies in the mutual interpenetration of the human and the divine.

The poems of Fray Luis were first published forty years after his death by Quevedo, who hoped their influence would check the modish flood of poetry in the manner of Góngora. This event of

1631 could serve to remind us that the Baroque Age was not after all the Age of the Counter Reformation. The two are indeed prominently joined in most general histories of art, architecture and religion, but it requires little sensibility to feel a profound disharmony between the two: between the ascetic spirit of Ignatius, Caraffa, Pius V on the one hand, and on the other the most voluptuous, theatrical style in the whole art history of the West. Did not the first mark a reaction against the High Renaissance, the second a resumption of its quest for glory?

The style ready to hand and used by sixteenth-century founders was that we now call Mannerism, the somewhat flaccid and ambivalent descendant of Michelangelo's *maniera*. Whether we regard it as an effective style or as a mere failure of nerve, it can scarcely be judged a very apt vehicle for the religious message of revived Catholicism. As for the origins of the Baroque, they may doubtless be detected around 1600, yet the great Roman works enabling us to assess its scope are those of Bernini, Borromini and Pietro da Cortona, dating from the fourth decade of the seventeenth century. How different was this period from the Ignatian Age! And more different still were eighteenth-century Spain, Austria, Bavaria and Franconia, those settings wherein the Baroque reached its second great peak. It was the multi-purpose style of a worldly generation. The arts of flattery and glorification infused its every form. If it expressed some of the religious sentiments of that generation, it proved still better suited to the presentation of autocratic monarchies, including those of Louis XIV and the Austrian Habsburgs.

Yet if this be so, how do we explain the striking use of the Baroque by the religious Orders, especially by the Jesuits, the Oratorians, the Theatines in those great Roman churches which set a pattern for the rest of Christendom? Here Mr Haskell and other historians of patronage have discovered a situation unexpectedly intricate. In the seventeenth century all these Orders had become part of a secure establishment, patronized by popes, cardinals and nobles, their individual characteristics obscured within a society more affluent and less disturbed than that of their early days. The *Imago Primi Sæculi*, that superb centenary volume published at Antwerp by

98 Title-page of the Jesuit
Imago Primi Sæculi
(Antwerp 1640)

99 Bernini's *Ecstasy of St Teresa*
in the Cornaro Chapel,
S. Maria della Vittoria, Rome
(1644–52). See p. 170 and
compare with
ill. 95 ▶

the Jesuits in 1640, would doubtless have shocked St Ignatius, as it shocked contemporaries, by its vainglorious *esprit de corps*. More important still, during the period of Bernini and Borromini (both d. 1667) the religious Orders themselves had little control over the decoration of their churches. As for the Gesù, the Vallicella of the Oratorians, and S. Andrea della Valle of the Theatines, their main structures had been built by cardinal-patrons in the Mannerist period. When they came to be embellished in the Baroque style and their famous side-chapels created, the extraneous patronage became still more marked, the influences still further secularized. This costly idiom demanded the wealth of Roman prelates and noble families; their money decided the artistic issues, and the officials of the Orders can be shown to have taken little part in the decisions. In these resplendent buildings we behold a reflection, not of the founder-saints of the mid sixteenth century, but of a rich aristocracy in whose minds a pietized neo-Renaissance spirit still held sway.

That tensions ensued we cannot doubt. In 1611 the eminent Jesuit Louis Richeôme dedicated a book to his general, Aquaviva; it denounced an extravagant profusion of columns, pilasters and volutes as irrelevant to Christian devotions, and it urged that paintings in churches should deliver plain sermons to their beholders. This opinion came as a harsh and disregarded voice from the heroic past. There arrived indeed other Jesuits who linked the images of ecclesiastical art with the imagery of meditation as taught by St Ignatius, yet their views seem at best peripheral to the intent of the founder. In their uses of contemporary art the Jesuits were in general less knowledgeable and discerning than were the Oratorians; it is hard to resist the impression that most of them were busy, functional, missionizing men with little time for the finer points of taste, the subtler relations between art and religion. And if the plans of their churches were commonly referred to the general in Rome, this does not mean that a special 'Jesuit style' adorned the landscapes of Catholic Europe. Writing of Baroque in Spain, Mr Lees-Milne remarks that 'a conflicting variety of styles characterized the façades and interiors of Spanish Jesuit as well as of non-Jesuit churches.'

100 Francesco Borromini, perhaps the most original of all Baroque architects, created the spire of S. Ivo della Sapienza, Rome, in 1642–50

101, 102, 103 Top left, the Mannerist façade of S. Andrea della Valle, begun 1594 and completed largely by Maderna. Top right, the design by Rughesi for the façade of S. Maria in Vallicella, completed 1605. Below, the Gesù, built 1568–75 by Vignola and della Porta by order of Cardinal Alessandro Farnese ▶

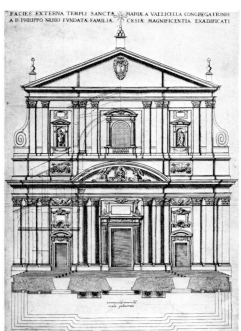

Thinking more broadly, it would seem indiscriminate to deny a spiritual character to Baroque art. Even at its most mawkish, it has appealed to simple but well-conditioned minds. At its greatest, as in the work of that gloomy, introverted Lombard Francesco Borromini—whose intricate spatial relations never fail to dominate the mere décor—it attains one of the soaring peaks of European architecture. Here, however, is the abstract, original, intellectual wing of an art too often stereotyped on its more vulgar levels. But at every level the alleged derivation of the Baroque from Ignatian or Teresan spirituality can be critically disputed. Inspecting Bernini's famous group of Teresa and the Seraph in S. Maria della Vittoria, a distinguished sensualist is said to have observed, 'If that is divine love, it is very familar to me.' There are today many people whose image of the saint is based on this Baroque *tour de force*, but they must surely be people who have never read her autobiography or the *Interior Castle*. In short, the Baroque was not a hymn of joy on the lips of reforming saints: even at its most religious it was a pantheon erected by a later age to commemorate dead heroes, whose inner lives were not accurately remembered.

As the Catholic Reformation breathed life into languishing art forms and modes of devotion, so it performed a similar service for scholastic theology and philosophy. The revival of Thomism before and during the Council of Trent came at a favourable moment, when the limitations of humanist speculative thought had become apparent, but before the new worlds of Galileo and Descartes had been revealed. While the Dominicans professed a 'pure' and conservative approach to the great master of their own Order, the Jesuits essayed more free and humane interpretations of St Thomas. The greatest of the latter was Francisco de Suarez (1548–1617), who elaborated structures broadly similar to those of Thomism, but departed from the latter on certain important issues, such as that of congruent grace. Here Suarez, standing close to his fellow Jesuit Luis de Molina (d. 1600), proposed an ingenious solution to the dichotomy between human free will and divine grace which still attracts the non-Thomist theologians of the Catholic Church. Suarez was no mere academic thinker. His work *De Legibus* (1612) set forth the principles of natural and international law, obtaining wide influence among jurists throughout Europe. His *Defensio Fidei* (1613), attacking the Church of England, was not merely burned in London but banned by the Parlement of Paris, because it assigned too little authority to the secular state. Even between themselves the Jesuits and the Dominicans were engaged in no mere mock-combat. Molina and his Dominican adversary Bañez (d. 1604) still arouse interest through the acuteness of their thought on those problems of man's freedom and God's omnipotence which remain central to philosophical theology.

The lively character of this world is again illustrated by another great Jesuit, St Robert Bellarmine (1542–1621), who combined a life of outstanding devotion with great analytical and expository powers. His *Disputationes de Controversiis* (1586–93) served many generations as a compendium of the Catholic positions in the contest with Protestantism, and attracted some two hundred rejoinders. While an upholder of the Thomist approach, Bellarmine saw clearly that the Church could not maintain its credibility through syllogisms alone, and that its champions must rival the Protestants in the fields of Church history and textual criticism. Of the many famous clashes of his career perhaps the most significant was that with the proto-Jansenist Baius, in which the Jesuit strove to demonstrate how the freedom of the will remains unimpaired even as it submits to the power of efficacious grace. One need hardly add that this contention also assaulted the Lutheran and Calvinist positions. On the other side Bellarmine was no creature of that papal extremism which hankered after political dominion; with Sixtus V he fell into disgrace for holding that the pope had only an indirect, not a direct power in the temporal affairs of the world.

It is usual but not wholly fair to label men like Bellarmine, Cano, Maldonatus and even Suarez as neo-scholastics. They were also distinguished writers who profited fully from humanist modes of expression; they were not slavish commentators on Aristotle or Aquinas. Within its limits their period was one of progress, which sought not to perpetuate but to abandon the useless subtleties of a decadent scholasticism. Nevertheless, they had only a short period of grace before the onset of new and compelling movements in philosophy. Even in their heyday there had developed that scepticism towards universal syntheses, that distaste for precise verbal ratiocination so well illustrated by Montaigne (*Essais*, 1580, 1588). Neo-scholasticism achieved momentum only on the eve of Cartesian thought and of the dramatic succession of discoveries in the natural sciences which had a cumulative effect on all philosophical and theological systems. The age of the telescope and the microscope did not necessarily disprove the conclusions of scholastic thinkers, but it made their approach look dry, abstract and academic. In addition, the scholastics of the seventeenth century made little serious attempt to incorporate the new world-picture into their systems. To their critics they seemed to be disregarding the clear evidence of the senses; in effect they allowed scholastic thought to be driven behind the walls of seminaries and houses of religion, there to form a hieratic cult unshared by the priesthood with the laity. A further and cruder factor contributed to the decline of scholasticism as the seventeenth century advanced: the majority of its recent champions had been Spaniards, and their repute suffered along with the political decline of Spain.

If the function of this essay were merely to provide accounts of saints and founders of communities, it would at this point remain little more than half completed. As yet we have scarcely touched upon the first half of the seventeenth century, a period exceptionally rich in such figures, a period when France, hitherto on the margins of the Catholic Reformation, suddenly became its main focus. In the history of French religion, the heart of the *Grand Siècle* is the reign of Louis XIII, not that of his son. Even during the reign of Henry IV its glories could hardly have been predicted. To see the preceding period of civil war as one of germination is easier for learned historians than it could have been for contemporary Frenchmen. Capuchin houses multiplied, while among the Cistercians the Abbé Jean de la Barrière set up his austere rule (1577) in the house at Les-Feuillans near Toulouse. Brought by Henry III to a building near the Tuileries, the 'Feuillans' thenceforth played a striking role in the religious life of the capital.

During the last years of the century the chief strongholds of Catholic piety lay in Provence, at Avignon, Arles, Saint-Rémy, Cavaillon and Aix, places where it seems to have enveloped people in all walks of life and where it was undoubtedly stimulated by the intimate contacts binding Provence with Italy. In this area the cousins César de Bus and Jean-Baptiste Romillon founded in 1592 the Congregation of Christian Doctrine, an Order mainly dedicated to plain religious teaching for both adults and children. These men, who certainly learned some of their methods from Jesuits, are interesting chiefly as precursors. When in 1605 de Bus proposed the taking of actual vows, the Order began to fall apart. Those of its members who rejected vows joined the Oratorians in 1619 and paved the way for the work of Bérulle.

Meanwhile, a remarkable number of Jesuit colleges had made their appearance in France, but their progress received a rude check when in 1594 a former pupil of the Collège de Clermont tried to assassinate Henry IV. The enemies of the Society of Jesus took this opportunity to procure the brutal closure of many of its establishments, and their restoration was delayed until 1603. Thereafter Jesuit influence continued to expand apace, and a high proportion of Frenchmen eminent in every field had their training in Jesuit schools.

The French Counter Reformation proved nevertheless a many-sided movement and one in no sense dominated by the Society. Many of its strands united in the person of St François de Sales (1576–1622), heir of Augustine and Aquinas, of the *Imitation*, of Christian humanism, of St Teresa. In his turn he could claim a large share in the inspiration of nearly every French evangelical movement of his day. By the time he attained his thirty-second year this great Savoyard had become famous for his exploits in reconverting—against every human and material obstacle—a large part of the Calvinist population of Chablais. Succeeding to the titular bishopric of Geneva, he made his headquarters at Annecy a centre of intense missionary effort. He ardently desired to save those many who had to live in the world and therefore thought the devout life beyond their powers. He preached indefatigably, wrote thousands of letters to his disciples and published two immensely

104 Emblem of
St François de Sales
described below

influential books, *Introduction to the Devout Life* (1608), and the more advanced *Treatise of Divine Love* (1616). A serene spirit who had overcome a dark phase of doubt in his earlier years, he taught enthusiasts how to lose their self-regard, to go about their duties with good sense, to discipline themselves in a middle path. The author of a popular book of emblems, *La Vie Symbolique du bienheureux François de Sales* (1664), epitomized his teaching in the picture of a sailing-boat crossing stormy waters between two great rocks; the superscription reads: MEDIUM TENUERE BEATI.

Above all St François afforded guidance to many of the remarkable women who were now playing major parts in the French revival. First among these was a noble widow of heroic energy, Jeanne de Chantal, who in 1610 established the Congregation of the Visitation. It was intended for women who, though unfitted to extreme austerities, wanted to embrace an active rule of service and charity. Through the incomprehension of the archbishop of Lyons the founders were virtually forced to turn it into a contemplative Order, but it flourished on this level and at the death of St Jeanne in 1641 there were already in existence eighty-six houses of the Visitation. Another pupil of St François was Angélique Arnauld (1591–1661), when she was still the young reforming abbess of Port-Royal. Under his direction she sought to enter the Visitation, but in the year of his death she was refused permission by Rome

174

and fell under the very different guidance of the Abbé de Saint-Cyran (d. 1643). A former fellow student of Jansen, he was the leading French champion of the emphases based upon St Augustine which we reviewed both in relation to Luther and to the Catholic Augustinians of the mid sixteenth century. Through his influence Port-Royal embarked upon those long and sensational vicissitudes of fame, holiness and persecution, which led to the destruction of the community in 1709.

In his earlier years François de Sales had himself been influenced by yet another famous lady, Madame Acarie (d. 1618), into whose circle in the Faubourg Saint-Antoine he was received during his visit to Paris in 1602. This group has amusing if superficial resemblances to the *salons* of the *précieuses*, yet of its quality and its ultimate effectiveness there can be no doubt. Deeply affected by reading a life of St Teresa, and herself a recipient of visions and ecstasies, Madame Acarie had undertaken the task of extending the Carmelite Order in France. Later on she similarly furthered the growth of the French Ursulines and encouraged Bérulle with his adaptation of the Oratory to French needs. Cardinal Bérulle (1575–1629) stands among the seminal personalities of the Gallic Counter Reformation. On the one hand he was a cool and patient negotiator, famous for helping to arrange the marriage of Charles I and Henrietta Maria, and for

105 *St François with St Jeanne de Chantal,* by Noel Hallé (d. 1781)

reconciling Louis XIII with one of the more troublesome mothers ever to afflict a sovereign. On the other hand he harboured a masterful conviction that the prime need of the French Church was the need for an educated and spiritually formed parish clergy. It had proved easy to decree seminaries at Trent, harder to get them actually founded, hardest of all to find men who could breathe life into them. Around the year 1600 and for some decades afterwards a multitude of witnesses testify that in France the cause of reform had exerted singularly little effect upon parish priests and their flocks. It was not without reason that in Provence and elsewhere people were still heard saying, 'If you want to go to hell, make yourself a priest.' Here was the old anticlericalism made harsher by continued hardship and neglect. Bérulle's initial success proved limited, but he made an important advance in setting his Oratorians to work, not like the Jesuits as a picked body of shock-troops, but in a more prosaic fashion among and alongside the parish priests. In his last years he responded to papal pressure and began also to found schools, a step which involved direct disputes with the Jesuits.

Under Charles de Condren (d. 1641), Bérulle's able successor as superior-general, the French Oratorians gradually extended their own influence and inspired others to found further seminaries, like the famous one established by Condren's disciple Jean-Jacques Olier at Saint-Sulpice, those associated with St Jean Eudes, and those founded by the Lazarists under the guidance of St Vincent de Paul (c. 1580–1660). The last-named could be considered the final great saint of the Counter Reformation; perhaps he has remained the most popular and best remembered of them all. His story is that of a 'natural' man of religion; one whose transparent goodness and boundless energy affected the most hardened and embittered minds. It is hard to think of an unsympathetic element in Monsieur Vincent, unless it be his uncompromising dislike of Jansenism, for he was one of those who worked hard for its condemnation. After an adventurous early life—which included his capture by the Barbary corsairs and his sale as a slave in Tunis—he came under the influences of Cardinal Bérulle and François de Sales, finding in the end not one single vocation but several in parallel.

106 St Vincent de Paul discussing with the Ladies of Charity the raising of funds for their Foundling Hospital ▶

His efforts developed along three main lines: missions to the people, the training of the secular clergy, and the relief of suffering, but all three were rigorously governed by the central motive of conversion to Christ. Already Jesuits like Auger in the south, Régis in Velay, Véron around Caen and La Nobletz in Brittany, had been pioneers of the rural mission. Vincent de Paul, and soon after him St Jean Eudes, were the first to organize such missions upon a national scale. Vincent founded the Congregation of the Mission in 1625; seven years later it was papally ratified and took over the disused leper hospital of Saint-Lazare. Called Lazarists in France, Italy and England, *padres paules* in Spain and later on Vincentians in America, the priests of the Mission had fifty-three houses by 1700 and then grew more slowly to the Revolution. Their original purpose was limited to country missions, and with this end in view Vincent carefully trained them to discard all traces of fashionable eloquence and speak in terms intelligible to the peasantry. From his room in Saint-Lazare, the commander-in-chief directed over eight hundred regional missions by steady streams of letters and instructions.

The recorded utterances of Vincent de Paul continually revert to one theme: 'Christianity depends on the priests. . . . Priests living in the manner most do today, are the greatest enemies of God's Church. . . . There is nothing so grand as a good priest.' His scheme of retreats for ordinands, first concerted in 1628, was soon taken over by the archbishop of Paris and then by a good third of the dioceses of France. Both these and his famous 'Tuesday Conferences' for secular clergy might not unfairly be described as crash-courses, and the need to expand the meagre number of seminaries remained. Their steady multiplication in Paris and the provincial cities gave a new direction to the work of the Lazarists. By the time of Vincent's death some four hundred priests were annually issuing from his colleges. The organization of the latter marked some real advances on that of their predecessors. The Council of Trent had left it to be assumed that twelve-year-old boys should be admitted to the same seminaries as adult students. In such institutions as those erected by St Charles Borromeo in Milan or by the cardinal of Lorraine at Rheims, or even in those of Bérulle's Oratorians, this admixture had not proved successful and it was left to Vincent's common sense to divide them into 'major' and 'minor' seminarists, and to train them in separate institutions. He took the view, liberal for those days, that the boy-entrants should not be held under obligation to enter the priesthood against their will. In none of these places can the training be regarded as comparable with that afforded by their modern equivalents. It varied in length, but in general below a maximum of two years. Highly disciplined in terms of prayer and fasting, it gave only a minimum of intellectual training, yet it produced generations of parish priests far more effective than their predecessors.

Ceaselessly practical in his benevolence towards the poor and the sick, the foundlings, the galley-slaves, the victims of war and hunger, Vincent did more than any man of his age to present Christianity as a religion of love. In 1617, while still the obscure parish priest at Châtillon-des-Dombes, he began to organize the Ladies of Charity to work among the poor and the sick. Soon afterwards he established branches of the movement in other places,

107 Both Callot and the brothers Le Nain illustrate the social problems of seventeenth-century France: *Beggars at a Doorway* by Louis Le Nain (d. 1648)

and it extended to noble and wealthy women of the court: the queen herself was known to visit hospitals and minister to the patients. Charity became fashionable, and this in itself speaks volumes if comparison be made with the nobility of the previous century. Yet Vincent was never satisfied with token contributions, and the way to a more effective social Christianity was soon suggested to him by the saintly widow Louise de Marillac, whom he had appointed to inspect the work of the Ladies of Charity in the provinces. In 1633 they decided to recruit country girls brought up to hard labour and irksome tasks. For these Daughters of Charity Vincent wrote some of his most moving addresses, in which he makes clear the true singleness of an apparently dual task, one which he defines as: 'To give oneself to God in order to serve him in the person of the poor.' Never before had women of the people been given a chance to serve humanity upon this scale, and appropriately enough the Daughters of Charity—long called the Grey Sisters from their

108 *Punishments*, pen-and-ink study by Callot for the series *The Miseries of War* (1633)

original habit—are to this day the most numerous religious institute for women. Soon they were found in every place where charitable action was demanded: in hospitals and schools, amid the victims of war, famine and epidemics, even in the galleys and on the battlefields. When some pompous person lauded to Napoleon the new philanthropy of the Age of Enlightenment, the emperor cut him short with the words: 'All that is well and good, gentlemen, but give us a Grey Sister any time.'

In the days of Vincent de Paul the eighteen million people of France afforded a daunting challenge to the bravest of missionaries and social workers. It was a sprawling country of poor communications and divisive class-structure. If a heavy-handed government did not collect taxes very efficiently, it found local famines beyond its limited powers. We might suitably imagine the French people less in terms of aristocratic portraiture, more in terms of the peasant-groups by the brothers Le Nain, or in those of the sinister, meticulous engravings of Callot, with their beggars, pedlars and mountebanks, their poor criminals broken on the wheel or festooned from trees as food for the birds of prey. Missionary priests did not need to leave for China or Peru. Readers of Henri Bremond's classic *Histoire Littéraire du Sentiment Religieux en France* may well have come away with an impression of aristocratic ladies practising exquisite devo-

109 Georges de la Tour (d. 1652) painted his masterpieces in the provincial calm of Lunéville: *St Irene with St Sebastian*, now in the church of Broglie, Eure ▶

tional routines and enjoying a privileged access to divine grace. On the contrary, amid that inequitable and brutal world, the Catholic revival was a movement relatively well balanced and socially diffused. Whatever may have been the case in former times, the Church now stood—and was seen to stand—for more humane and merciful ideals than did civil society. If once again he may seek to epitomize the world of the spirit in the visual image, the writer finds a wealth of meaning in the works of the Lorraine painter Georges de La Tour (d. 1652), the strange, still beauty of which has been rediscovered in our own century. Are these not the truest emblems of the last creative phase in the Catholic Reformation?

XII DISCUSSION

It must be acknowledged that the Counter Reformation was deeply divided: vertically by national and regional responses, horizontally by the great variety of the actions comprised. The story of crusading Spain, that of neo-Franciscan Italy, that of the Netherlands still enthralled by the *devotio moderna*; how much safer it would be to describe these separately rather than as parts of a greater whole! And as for the horizontal divisions, do they not cover every activity, from the higher mysticism down to disciplinary measures worthy of a police state? What links existed between official policies and the spontaneous love of God? Should we place the Spanish Carmelites among the creators or among the victims of the 'movement'? Upon which common denominators should most stress be laid? Even when we speak of the defence and teaching of Catholic doctrine, how precisely can the latter be defined in terms applicable to all those *dramatis personae* normally counted as Catholics?

We have tried to explain that even the developed Counter Reformation was far from being purely a movement directed against Protestantism. It also involved definition, hispanicizing, universalism and the suppression of interior tensions. Many issues hitherto obscure and subject to academic debate were sharply defined. For a time the reduced Church came under harsh pressures from Spain, until recently an outward-turning frontier with little influence upon medieval Christendom. Again, it was a period when the Papacy curbed its Italian state-building only to press with greater vigour its old claims to universal authority. With equal significance, the story also includes the victory of papal monarchy and Tridentine principles over a series of internal oppositions: Gallicanism, conciliarism, Augustinianism, biblical humanism and ecumenism. So regarded, the movement hinges upon the last session of the Council of Trent, since not until then did the Papacy and its allies cohere in effective action. Before 1563 we see many tributaries but no single mighty river.

That the Trent settlement proved doctrinally durable, one cannot question. With some justification, its spirit is often said to have lasted until our own day, at least to the pontificate of John XXIII and the Second Vatican Council. Yet pressed too far, this view simplifies Catholic history since Trent. The whole modern history of the Church does not spring either from a unique revival of the sixteenth century, or from a single response to the traumatic shock administered by Luther and Calvin. It contains a whole series of revivals and a whole series of responses to a long succession of shocks occasioned by scepticism, scientism, rationalism, anticlericalism, liberal democracy, theological modernism, socialism and communism. Around the period of the Revolution, most of the old heresies showed themselves to have survived all attempts at extirpation. Then for Protestants and Catholics alike, the nineteenth century was an age of turbulent change resulting both in revivals and in losses. Altogether, the specialists on Reformation and Counter Reformation sometimes attribute too much of our present religious landscapes to the earthquakes of the sixteenth century.

However durable many aspects of the settlement, we have here considered the Counter Reformation, properly so called, to have terminated around the middle of the seventeenth century, a time of spiritual cooling and many non-Catholic trends. Already in the Rome of Urban VIII and Bernini one may perceive a substitute-Renaissance. Reserved, sometimes illiberal in its attitudes towards fundamental thinking on man and the universe, the Roman Church made more than a little concession to that love of theatricality and splendour ineradicable from Italian minds. It proclaimed that if these things submitted themselves, however perfunctorily, to the demands of institutional religion, then men were permitted to enjoy them also. The Counter Reformation thus lost its creative religious tensions not only amid the rise of scepticism but by permission of a cultured establishment, which was content to mime the original drama. Yet this slackening of the seventeenth century does not mean that the tensions of the sixteenth had failed to leave

183

permanent marks upon the Church and upon Catholic society. If the saints slept, at least they did not die. In Goethe's famous phrase, 'all greatness is educative'.

'No great book, that is one which reveals man more profoundly to man, was inspired by the Counter Reformation. Nor did any poet do this, not even Torquato Tasso.' So Croce bewailed what he took to be cultural decline from the peak of the High Renaissance. Yet as Koenigsberger has recently argued, what we find during the Age of Counter Reformation is not cultural decline but cultural shift. Admittedly, the growing limitations upon political liberty and freedom of expression blighted Italian political and social thought. But in music, architecture and painting, the most illustrious figures abounded in great numbers throughout the period of Counter Reformation, most numerously in Rome itself. That period also coincided with many masterpieces of Spanish literature, especially with those of the classical theatre, one of whose greatest figures Pedro Calderon was not only a priest, but earned the soubriquet 'poet of the Inquisition'.

The relations of the natural sciences to the Counter Reformation afford some complexities. It would seem that, throughout most fields, the work of Spanish scientists did in the long run suffer enfeeblement through the narrowing orthodoxy of the age. Regarding their Italian contemporaries even so guarded a generalization would be far too sweeping. The attempt to suppress Galileo displays a truly obscurantist spirit which shocked Catholic as well as non-Catholic men of learning throughout Europe. Yet it cannot be taken as evidence that Papacy and Inquisition blasted scientific thinking as a whole. In any general work on seventeenth-century scientific discoveries, the reader will assuredly find a host of important Italian names. In general, their work was not done furtively, and scientific academics arose under official patronage. The Accademia dei Lincei was founded in Rome by Prince Cesi in 1603, the Accademia del Cimento by Ferdinand II, grand duke of Tuscany, half a century later, but still in advance of the English Royal Society. All in all, in so far as any decline occurred in Mediterranean culture, it was less the direct result of the religious

Counter Reformation than of its Baroque mimics who developed its repressive mechanisms while losing its spiritual resources.

A related topic to be handled with even greater caution is the claim that Reformation and Counter Reformation divided Europe into two separate cultures. However we may define a 'culture', this notion is hard to accept even in relation to activities within or near the religious sphere. To a surprising extent, the two sides continued to talk the same language. Whatever Luther may have said against Aristotelian philosophy and theology, the Lutheran world had fallen under their spell—equally with the Roman world—within a few decades of Luther's death. In 1598 Daniel Hoffmann was expelled from his professorial chair at Helmstedt for protesting against this situation. From about this date the Spanish neo-scholastics were quoted 'with almost canonical authority' in Lutheran textbooks on metaphysics. In virtually all the Lutheran universities the *Disputations* of Suarez became the handbook of scholastic metaphysics. The Calvinist Opitz (d. 1639) imitated Catholic poets and translated a work of Catholic propaganda. The Lutheran Gryphius (d. 1664) translated a Jesuit play; the Hamburg citizen Zesen and the Nuremberg patrician Harsdörffer, both Protestants, translated Catholic devotional literature. Johann Arndt, the forerunner of Pietism, is chiefly remembered on account of his *Four Books of the True Christianity* (1606), a work based on Tauler, the *Imitation*, Angela of Foligno and Raymond of Sebonde.

It would be as easy to list connections of this type between England—allegedly so insular, so Protestant—and the culture of Counter-Reformation Europe. Between 1582 and 1604 some twenty-three editions of works by Luis de Granada appeared in the English language, over half of them published not by Catholic émigrés but in London. Between Elizabeth's accession and 1640 there were over thirty English editions of the *Imitation*, nearly all published in London. In 1582 Robert Parsons, the Jesuit leader of militant English Catholicism, published at Rouen his *Book of Christian Exercises;* two years later the Calvinist-Anglican cleric Edmund Bunny set forth a version of Parsons adapted for Protestant use and this became so popular as to run into twenty editions. Apart from these, the second part of Parsons's book was anonymously adapted to Protestant use and attained ten more editions. Likewise in the mid seventeenth century the Protestant schoolmaster Charles Hoole recommended the standard Jesuit Latin grammar for use in English schools, while the Puritan John Dury, a *protégé* of Comenius, praised as educational models the Jesuit colleges he had seen on the Continent. Italian literature became the staple fare of the better educated among the Elizabethan gentry, while for those lacking the gift of tongues, there abounded translations of Italian and Spanish works of all types. Later on and throughout the eighteenth century a period of residence in Catholic countries formed the taste of the English aristocracy. Many of these, like the convinced Anglican Sir Thomas Browne, freely worshipped in Catholic churches when abroad; numerous others and their descendants breathed the very spirit of Catholic Europe in the works of art they brought back from the Continent.

The political fears and Protestant bigotry of the English did not prevent their Stuart kings from marrying Catholic princesses. Their metaphysical poets imitated Góngara and the Marinisti. William Harvey's discovery of the circulation of the blood was by no means unconnected with his study and graduation in Galileo's Padua, while Milton's stay in Italy and his knowledge of her literature supplied him with creative influences of the first order. Both Bellarmine and the neo-scholastics became extremely familiar to English theologians; Bellarmine himself kept in his room a portrait of William Whitaker of Cambridge, as the most learned of all his

110 Emblem adapted 1635 by Francis Quarles from a Jesuit original (at right) of 1629

Lord all my desire is before thee and my groaning is not hid from thee. Ps: 38

Domine, ante te omne desiderium meum, et gemitus meus a te non est absconditus. Psal. 37.

111 Netherlandish still-life, Italianate Baroque and Catholic eucharistic piety all unite in J. de Heem, *The Eucharist*, 1648

adversaries. These instances and scores of others concern Protestant Englishmen: needless to add, many English Catholics, both *émigrés* and home-lovers, attained still more intimate relations with the culture of Catholic countries. No one wrote more splendidly of St Teresa than did the convert Richard Crashaw.

Similar schemes could be elaborated for the United Provinces. Even upon their highly indigenous painting, Italian influences could become profound, as in the cases of the Utrecht school and the predecessors of Rembrandt. The very costume of the Dutch regent class was based upon that of their Spanish enemies. As for France, it can hardly be said that at any stage religion divided her into cultural zones, even though she had lain for so many decades in tension between the poles of Paris and Geneva. Symbolically, Jean-Baptiste Romillon while still a young Huguenot soldier was given the copy of Luis de Granada which began his conversion to Catholicism. And when the pamphleteers of the Catholic League wanted to justify the deposition of Henry IV, they avidly borrowed the arguments and texts hitherto directed by the *Vindiciae contra Tyrannos* and other Huguenot writings against Catholic monarchs. Later on, Richelieu left both his public and his private finances in the hands of allegedly Protestant bankers, who sustained with businesslike detachment the main opposing contenders in the Thirty Years War. Richelieu's own pet aversion was not Huguenotism, which he attacked merely on political grounds, but the Spanish ideal of the *hidalgo*. One of his leading ambitions was to erect trading companies on the model of the so-called Calvinist Dutch. The new science, Cartesian philosophy and Baroque art were not the only types of fashion to overleap religious boundaries. For example, that wave of puritanism which in the 1620s attacked stage-plays, gay clothes and tavern life, was also noticeable in Spain and in Bavaria, in which latter it rivalled all the Protestant manifestations. Without any surprise, one finds it too among the Jansenists; and if this spirit be correctly called puritanism, Archbishop Laud himself was a puritan as well as a persecutor of Puritans.

All in all, Reformation and Counter Reformation did not lead even temporarily to the creation of two separate cultures. This was one world rather than two. Nevertheless, the reader will have noticed that the great majority of these influences flowed in one direction: from Catholic into Protestant Europe. Perhaps this fact does not denote inferiority in the latter so much as archaism and complacency in the former. The pride and passionate orthodoxy of Spain, the lingering conviction of Italians that other nations were barbarians, these had become cultural and economic liabilities by the mid seventeenth century, when both countries had now so much to learn from northern Europe.

Like all major religious movements, the Counter Reformation was to some extent modified, even deflected by secular forces. We have observed its protagonists finding their political allies in Spain and Portugal, in the Habsburgs and the Wittelsbachs, in the surviving prince-bishops of central Europe, in the Italian states dominated by Spanish and papal influence. As for France, the ambivalent foreign policy of her rulers had political origins, for their hostility towards internal Protestantism remained fairly consistent up to the Revolution. Of all these political associates the Habsburgs, and especially the Spanish Habsburgs, proved the most dangerous to the health of the religious movement: this happened in part because their self-deception included so much sincerity. The more Catholicism seemed indebted to them, the less was its chance of reconquering Protestant peoples—and the less healthy its situation in France. Throughout Europe, friend and foe, Catholic and Protestant, remained all too aware of the Habsburg tendency to manipulate both Rome and the new Catholicism for dynastic ends. Most of the popes were equally aware that the blows of the enemy might be less noxious than the infected kiss of a friend.

The sociology of the Counter Reformation has not yet been adequately explored. The substantial support given by social and economic discontents to various phases of the Protestant Reformation is a more familiar if still debatable subject. On the other hand, it must be conceded that the European society of that day also contained many social forces and popular attitudes making for religious conservatism. Aware of its limited recuperative powers and educated by its occasional glimpses of chaos, sixteenth-century society valued law and order. Sometimes peasants rioted, but in general they were patient creatures. Unless subjected to violent innovations or exceptional propaganda they growled over their grievances yet continued with their vital tasks. As the century advanced, peasant malcontents received increasing proof that they were no match for professional soldiers. And whereas urban populations were capable of political, even religious thinking, peasants still tended to expect leadership from their clergy and their landlords.

In town and country alike, economic and social malaise was balanced by the restraints of a society in which the vast majority was conditioned to acknowledge hierarchy and degree. Over large stretches of Europe, feudal habits of mind had as yet suffered little disturbance; for example, the complex religious history of Poland followed the responses of the great landowners, who broadly speaking determined the confessional allegiances of their tenants. Everywhere in Europe the work of the Jesuits could be lightened by a sympathetic aristocracy as well as by favourable governments.

Any exhaustive study of social and religious conservatism would also need to collect evidence concerning the non-economic attitudes of the people. On the one hand prophecies and millenarian lore sometimes encouraged rebellions; on the other, the all-too-frequent epidemics, famines, natural disasters were widely attributed to the wrath of God against disobedient and heretical peoples. In addition, however weighty the evidence for anticlericalism, the fact remains that parish priests and preachers, normally though not universally religious conservatives, remained the regular channels through which ideas reached rural society.

Those who reaped immediate secular profits from the Counter Reformation did not usually include the nobility and gentry. Unlike the Protestant Reformation, it did nothing to assuage the land-hunger of laymen. In Protestant countries the ruling classes flourished together with the parliaments they managed, but their equivalents suffered badly in Spain, where so many aristocrats were reduced to poverty, or to service abroad under the Crown. Philipine Spain was notoriously the land of 'closed palaces'. Yet it must be added that in the longer run the preserved Church, like most of its Protestant rivals, formed a pillar of social stability and traditional landlordism.

Medieval civilization had produced two potential agencies of 'free' and 'progressive' thought: the universities and the self-governing cities. In some parts of Europe both had shown strong tendencies to embrace the Protestant Reformation, the Catholic adversaries of which had thus no reason to love academic or civic independence. On the whole these freedoms seem accordingly to have been diminished by the Counter Reformation. A university in Jesuit hands or under the eye of the Inquisition did not enjoy much freedom. Neither did a city under the Interim of Augsburg. Nevertheless, the drift to autocracy came largely from secular sources. And after all, Protestant princes also attacked municipal liberties, while Catholicism could not be taught at Wittenberg or Cambridge! In Italy the decline of the free cities and the rise of princely capitals had begun centuries before Reformation and Counter Reformation. This antithesis between free cities and court cities can indeed be overdrawn, while the losses to freedom, which almost everywhere had occurred in the fourteenth and fifteenth centuries, have been too commonly linked with the sixteenth; this apparently because of the two famous but quite exceptional survivals at Florence and at Venice. Nor should this antithesis be overstated in cultural terms. Princely capitals like Rome, Vienna, Munich and Salzburg—the last deliberately and splendidly developed by ecclesiastical princes as a little transalpine Rome—became in due course important cultural centres in their own right.

The most obvious secular beneficiaries of the Counter Reformation were the governments of the Catholic states. As individuals, their princes were not necessarily cynical exploiters of the religious movement. Like the Protestant rulers of the day, they form a miscellaneous assembly, including the sincerely religious and the paternally minded. But the so-called Renaissance state was no mere personal despotism. Its core and its substance lay in an expanded bureaucracy, the members of which stood together for mutual profit and were little restrained by modern notions of public service and ethics. On the whole it kept better order than the medieval state, but it tended to be both expensive and corrupt. In the Catholic lands, this top-heavy state became coupled in mutual support with an increasingly top-heavy Church, and however highly the latter's religious achievements may be assessed, the combination afflicted Catholic societies with an economic burden of increasing weight. In the classic case of Spain, the Inquisition became a financially profitable organ of government, while a hugely expanded ecclesiastical establishment created a large field of taxation for the king. Nevertheless, observers of that day and ever since have found in the Spanish Church one of those many factors which combined to produce an economic decline almost unparalleled in the history of any European nation. At all stages there have also been observers with so narrow a concept of Christianity as to admire without reserves this strange idealism, which seemingly strove to create a nation of soldiers, priests and monks. Yet in defence of the Catholic Reformation it should at least be argued that such was not the ambition of the great reformers, who did not envisage the creation of such a distorted society. As for the multiplication of Spanish monasteries, if it resulted from the ardours of the Catholic Reformation, it was a late result. It reached really alarming proportions only after 1600, when a growing religious mediocrity expressed itself in quantitative expansion. Meanwhile, the Cortes protested in vain against a process which any competent government could and would have checked.

The portion of Europe retained by Catholicism at first constituted well over a half, whether we assess it in terms of population, of wealth, of social and scientific thought, or of cultural creativity in general. But during the seventeenth century these balances gradually tipped, not simply towards Protestant countries but rather towards northern and western Europe as a whole, which also contained a large Catholic population. By the last decade of that century the competition for the leadership of the Continent and much of the extra-European world lay between France, where Catholicism was losing its grip upon the ruling classes, and a varied group of states politically comprising Austria but ideologically headed by England and the Netherlands, in both of which the stricter forms of Protestantism had lost their ascendancy. Her colonial empire apart, Spain was no longer a great power either politically or culturally; as for her religious example, it now inspired repulsion. But if Spain had become veritably exhausted, the plight of Italy was now more tragic; her still active and brilliant minds were compelled to think truths which censorship forced into silence or clandestine publication. Meanwhile, the seminal ideas of the new age were coming from Locke and Newton, to whom Voltaire and the *philosophes* of the Enlightenment would in due course succeed. While the Lutheran lands were now producing little save Pietism and great music, certain countries hitherto counted as Calvinist were already making, or were later to make, important contributions to Western culture.

When, however, this situation is investigated more narrowly, it does not support any simple-minded antithesis between a progressive Protestantism and a repressive Catholicism. By the early eighteenth century the intellectual leaders of Geneva, Amsterdam and Edinburgh were—like those of London—no longer controlled by Calvinist

112 The Spanish Inquisition remained active in the time of Goya (1746–1828), who made this sepia sketch of a penitent

ardour. As for the decline of Spain and Italy, a host of factors, mainly secular, have been found at work. What of the cramping hand of that church-state hybrid, the Inquisition? Here we have indeed no mere textbook fable. It cannot be cancelled from the list of truly retrogressive forces, yet on any credible analysis it must remain one among many. Catholic orthodoxy did not guarantee a relapse into political, economic or cultural sterility. Catholic Austria did not follow Spain into these doldrums; she was not unaffected by a reforming spirit and even the House of Habsburg managed to produce a passable imitation of a crowned Jacobin.

Throughout most of Europe a spirit had arisen by 1700 which did not necessarily discard Christianity, yet decisively rejected the type of idealism represented by Loyola and Calvin. If in many places religion continued lively, the strong currents of the eighteenth century washed it almost clean of dialectical matter, the dogmatic, scholastic grit of Reformation and Counter Reformation. The Society of Jesus lay suppressed from 1793 to 1814, the Sorbonne itself from 1792 to 1808; while the revival of scholastic studies was delayed until the last quarter of the nineteenth century.

193

Amid the din of battle, only quite exceptional men will calmly explore the enemy's ideology with a view to adopting its more attractive features. And who did more than the irascible Luther to create this din, this atmosphere of total warfare? Yet however we apportion the blame, embattled Catholicism missed considering Luther's creative contributions: his view of the functions of a vernacular liturgy; his concept of faith as *fiducia*, his feeling for lay participation and congregational community; his theocentric emphases arising from Paul and Augustine, his enlarged concept of a mysterious God, whose ways are not our ways. The Catholic Church took its chief anti-Augustinian decision not so much when it denounced Luther or discarded Contarini, Seripando and Baius, as when it decided to expel Jansenism with a fork. Yet as usual in such cases, this weapon scored only a partial success. By no means totally eradicated from France, a modified Jansenism migrated to Italy and achieved striking influence both upon the Enlightenment and within liberal Catholicism.

Again, however assiduously a Catholic biblical theology has been developed in recent times, it could scarcely be claimed that the Church of the Counter Reformation maintained with appropriate vigour the tradition of biblical humanism which it inherited. This tradition was not easily assimilated by a movement striving to recover ecclesiastical authority. In effect biblical humanism asserted that Christians must be intent to pursue the Christianity of Christ and his apostles; that this Christianity can only be verified by study of the original sources in the New Testament; that individual scholars armed with modern philological and historical techniques can make valid contributions to a Christianity thus progressively revealed to men. Such a conclusion clearly impinged upon the authority of pope and hierarchy as then envisaged. Moreover, it was soon extended to a still more challenging proposition: that if the biblical sources manifestly conflicted with ecclesiastical usages or with the presuppositions of scholastic theologians, it was not the biblical sources which the Church must throw aside.

From this point at least, biblical religion ran into harsher problems. The cry 'back to the Bible' may well seem more rational than, for example, the cry 'back to the Middle Ages', which has inspired so much romantic Catholicism and Anglo-Catholicism, as if it were somehow self-evident that the age of Innocent III and Aquinas provided the Christian norms. Yet while sixteenth-century exegesis made some solid advances, its techniques were still in the making; they were still inadequate to produce a fresh body of inescapable doctrine fit to be made obligatory by the Church. Such exegesis came not merely into the hands of humble scholars but into those of Protestants who combined debatable scholarship with monumental self-confidence and an officious zeal to apply their findings to the salvation of all men.

Catholic ecclesiastical authority not only feared the heresiarchs; it feared there would be as many sects as there were expositors. If in the event the popes and the Council tried to block this threat by authoritarian methods, the fault lay less with them than with the anxious, over-committed spirit of an age which did not fully under-stand the parable of the wheat and the tares. Despite the small and noble minority who taught a Gospel of gentleness and persuasion, the century following Luther and Loyola stood basically unprepared to practise free religious debate. The closed mind, the resort to juridical persecution, these were far from occurring exclusively within Catholic Europe.

The attempt to meet the high demands of the Gospel by with-drawal from society at large was common to Anabaptism and to orthodox monasticism. Sectarian withdrawal both strengthened and weakened Protestantism. But does not a similar critique apply to monastic withdrawal from Catholic society? The Catholic Reformation was characterized throughout by a proliferation of new religious Orders, even though some of these from the first modified the principle of withdrawal by that of practical service. This latter tendency we have duly described and applauded, yet we are still left wondering whether the very vitality of the new Orders may not in some measure have distracted Catholicism from its greatest practical problem: the need to train parish priests and hence provide the laity with better and more frequent Christian teaching. Did the spectacular charges of the cavalry cause the generals to neglect the weapons and training of their infantry? The conventional answer would be that no such dichotomy existed, and it could be in part supported by reference to those Orders which set out to support and ultimately to train the parish clergy. Yet there remains much evidence that these efforts, reinforced only by an uneven response to the Tridentine demand for seminaries, proved slow to take effect upon parish ministrations. And by the time real effects were widely forthcoming, was not the self-sufficiency of the Jesuits already weakening the relation between secular and regular clergy?

The great majority of Christian souls are those of parishioners. Catholicism seeks to bring them to God chiefly through divine grace as mediated in the sacraments and through the labours of its priesthood. In the sixteenth century the primary task of the Church lay in the rehabilitation of both clerical functions and the clerical image, especially those of the parish priest. Upon these actions depended the consolidation of any religious revival. The necessity was obvious to all thinking men in 1500: by 1600 the gains were widely appreciable, yet ample evidence suggests that even then they were slight in some areas of Europe. It seems at least arguable that if at all stages of the Catholic Reformation the best ordinands had not been drained off into the religious Orders, success might have come far sooner. And if for twenty years across the middle of the sixteenth century a great pope with a real knowledge of European society and a clear sense of priorities had occupied the throne of St Peter, then the campaign for the parochial ministry might have won its victories half a century earlier.

Needless to add, Protestant critics of that day tended to contrast the godly preacher with the Mass-priest who learned religion by rote; they connected any failure to provide a teaching clergy with an alleged Catholic over-emphasis upon the purely sacramental aspects of religion. Nevertheless, it remains doubtful whether the rural ministers of the Protestant churches made much swifter progress, and other explanations are to be preferred. Though the strengthening of episcopal powers was a major feature of the Catholic Reformation, there remained wide variations in the ability and the financial resources of actual bishops. Everywhere the magnitude and novelty of the task, the frequent lack of dynamic leadership both central and local, the dead hand of tradition in ecclesiastical finance and organization, the vagaries of lay patronage, the erosion of Church lands and tithes, the lack of obvious romantic appeal in the life of the secular priest, all these would seem more than enough to account for the gradual and uneven character of this vital process. But as it came to fruition, it transformed a too largely juridical approach to the laity into a more educational approach. How much better to teach laymen rather than burn them! This is a frequent clerical theme in both Catholic and Protestant circles from the early days of the confessional struggle.

It might hence be maintained that the Catholic advance experienced two notable delays which more imaginative leadership could have shortened. The first occupied the pontificates of Clement VII and Paul III; it sprang from the self-regarding timidity of the popes and the Curia. The other delay covered the two or three decades on each side of the year 1600; it arose from the slowness of the process whereby knowledge and integrity filtered downward to the parishes of Catholic Europe.

Non-Catholics have often reproached the Church which emerged from these events; they have denounced the absolutist spirit in which its jurisdiction was wielded, the tendency to equate a sin-laden historical Church with the immaculate Church of eschatology, its glorious pageantry and cautious clericalism, its past compromises with secular tyranny, its responsibility for those rigid and defensive attitudes which have lingered into our own day. But during the recent years marked by Pope John's *Aggiornamento* and the Second Vatican Council, thoughtful Catholics have often echoed these very criticisms. And if the claim to a unique authority must stand unchanged, it is nowadays proffered in very different terms. Officially the Catholic Church has denounced persecution of all types. It now bids its members respect other Churches as grace-bearing, other world religions as containing elements of the divine mind and purpose. All responsible Catholics accept in principle the rights of the individual conscience, even though in certain traditionalist countries the social and ecclesiastical pressures against nonconformity remain severe. Elsewhere 'liberal' criticism has rapidly developed within the Church, and it is directed against many features strengthened or at least spared by the Counter Reformation: against the superstitious notions all too easily arising from indulgences and the veneration of saints, against the danger that the ministrations of the Church may represent an 'externalized conscience', against an excessive concern with matters of technical and mechanical validity. And in our own day much avoidable suffering bids Catholics reconsider the validity of those arguments hitherto applied by the Church to the problems of contraception and over-population.

Whatever Trent may have said, many Catholic intellectuals doubt whether Aristotelian scholasticism can form an adequate basis for a Christian philosophy. Above all, informed Catholicism is anxious to avoid all impressions to the effect that the priesthood can capture, monopolize or manipulate the grace of God. Though in some countries the laity boldly claims an increased share in the administration of the Church, the liberalizing process is far from being centred upon this tendency. Resuming a movement we have witnessed in the sixteenth century, the bishops have now been assigned a higher role in ecclesiastical government, this principle of 'collegiality' entailing a proportionate decline in the powers of the Curia. Meanwhile, the Jesuits have recovered their capacity for large-scale thinking. Permitted a high measure of intellectual freedom, they sometimes champion causes which a few decades ago would have been considered dangerously opposed to their traditions.

The internal tensions produced by all these changes will be viewed with an unfeigned concern by everyone interested to preserve the influence of Christianity; the more so, since similar tensions have long beset most other forms of institutional religion. Yet it seems especially true of this world-wide multiracial Church that conflicting social and political forces throughout its many regions must inevitably invade its communal life and religious functions. Against these forces it cannot be fully immunized, nor can it avoid the further incompatibilities resulting from an unplanned world economy, ever at work to enrich the rich nations and to plunge the poor into new abysses of poverty. When sophisticated Catholic laymen complain that the role of 'a simple rustic piety' has hitherto been assigned them, they cannot remain unaware that the Church still contains millions of extremely simple rustics! In its rapid expansion throughout the world the Catholic Reformation inaugurated a huge experiment in interracial co-operation, the full significance of which has become apparent only in our own troubled century.

As the Counter Reformation becomes a historical memory rather than a governing principle of life, both Catholics and non-Catholics need to envisage it in a deeper perspective than that which satisfied their fathers and grandfathers. Historical memories are often more influential than they should be, and one task of the historian is to keep them under control. Both Reformation and Counter Reformation can remain sources of sterile tension if they become detached from the perspectives of their own age. Were not both movements grievously impaired by what now seem defective concepts of Christianity and of human values? Yet every age has martyred Christ's religion by means of its favourite instruments of torture, and our own, striving without conspicuous ability to avoid its nemesis, should not be over-censorious towards its predecessors. Even the stories of the inquisitor, the conquistador, the persecuting ruler, should be related to a historical context within which modern liberal values were only just beginning to find a foothold.

Those historians who systematically minimized the failings of the late medieval Church or of the Renaissance Papacy did a disservice to the Counter Reformation. In believing the Roman Church of his own day to be literally moribund, Luther admittedly went to an opposite extreme, yet he approached nearer to the truth than did the romantics who were dominating Church history only a few decades ago. The disciplinary oppressions pursued by some Counter-Reformation churchmen and their political backers are to be understood by reference to the profound gravity of a crisis with few real parallels in religious history. Yet such persecuting discipline seems most unlikely ever to be revived by Christians. Has it not now become the speciality of those who have made a religion of the secular state? Hence while historians must try to view the Counter

Reformation from every possible vantage-point, it may well be that their deeper interests will henceforth lie less along the political and ecclesiastical margins than within the field of religion proper.

Whatever its theological attitude towards the veneration of saints, a Church is above all a historical continuity, and without denying this essential attribute it cannot forget the splendours of its past. This seems equally true of Christianity as a whole, and its divided members can scarcely reunite save in the light of the whole Christian past. Catholicism from the conversion of Ignatius Loyola to the death of Vincent de Paul remains by any standards one of the classic chapters in the history of Christianity, a chapter inexhaustible in its fascinations and ever-rewarding in retrospect. Rightly or wrongly, the leaders of that age used rigorous methods to preserve a clearly defined structure comprising sacraments, creeds and ministry. With distinct narrowness but with a good measure of realism they emphasized the Christian community as opposed to the perils of individualism. Yet they also substituted missions for crusades and social concern for the pharisaic tasks of self-salvation. In a host of souls the Catholic Reformation fostered not merely obedience to the Church but also that spontaneous love of God which joyfully expresses itself in affection and service towards men.

Above the sombre valleys and prosaic plateaux, the mountain peaks rise in shining clusters towards the sun. In its saints many of us have found the permanent significance of the Catholic Reformation; and here we should be unwise to simplify our values in accordance with any one dramatic or fashionable model, such as that of the Spanish mystics. It may well be, for example, that some of the less mystical like Angela Merici or Vincent de Paul will have more effective uses for modern readers. All in all, these Catholic saints are a company of exceeding diversity and wealth. For one recent student at least it has been a delightful privilege even to observe them through a telescope from the territory of another tradition. They are indeed too good to remain the exclusive possession of the Church which bore and nourished them. In some sense their message serves not Catholics alone, but all men of good will: by such spiritual graces their exalted origins and destinies stand universally proclaimed.

THE POPES 1484–1655

INNOCENT VIII (Giambattista Cibò)   August 1484–July 1492

ALEXANDER VI (Rodrigo Borgia)   August 1492–August 1503

PIUS III (Francesco Todeschini-Piccolomini)   September–October 1503

JULIUS II (Giuliano della Rovere)   November 1503–February 1513

LEO X (Giovanni de' Medici)   March 1513–December 1521

ADRIAN VI (Adrian Dedel)   January 1522–September 1523

CLEMENT VII (Giulio de' Medici)   November 1523–September 1534

PAUL III (Alessandro Farnese)   October 1534–November 1549

JULIUS III (Giovanni Maria Ciocchi del Monte)   February 1550–March 1555

MARCELLUS II (Marcello Cervini)   April 9–30, 1555

PAUL IV (Gian Pietro Caraffa)   May 1555–August 1559

PIUS IV (Giovanni Angelo Medici)   December 1559–December 1565

PIUS V (Michele Ghislieri)   January 1566–May 1572

GREGORY XIII (Ugo Buoncompagni)   May 1572–April 1585

SIXTUS V (Felice Peretti)   April 1585–August 1590

URBAN VII (Giambattista Castagna)   September 15–27, 1590

GREGORY XIV (Niccolò Sfondrati)   December 1590–October 1591

INNOCENT IX (Giovanni Antonio Facchinetti)   October–December 1591

CLEMENT VIII (Ippolito Aldobrandini)   January 1592–March 1605

LEO XI (Alessandro Ottaviano de' Medici)   April 1–27, 1605

PAUL V (Camillo Borghese)   May 1605–January 1621

GREGORY XV (Alessandro Ludovici)   February 1621–July 1623

URBAN VIII (Maffeo Barberini)   August 1623–July 1644

INNOCENT X (Giambattista Pamfili)   September 1644–January 1655

Any short reading-list drawn from the enormous mass of printed materials on the Counter Reformation must be arbitrary. The books listed below are mostly recent and available in the libraries of the English-speaking world: some items are readable yet relatively slight, while many works of scholarly importance—including the collections of original sources—have had to be omitted. Wherever possible I give English translations of books originally published in other languages. Select bibliographies will be found, e.g., in the revised edition (1965) of H. J. Grimm, *The Reformation Era*, and in Dr Bossy's edition of Evennett, cited below. An interesting bibliographical survey is that by G. H. Tavard in *Church History*, xxvi (1957), pp. 275–88.

Books are published in London unless otherwise stated. [P] means available in paperback edition.

GENERAL ACCOUNTS

Burns, E. M. *The Counter Reformation* (Princeton 1964) [P]

Daniel-Rops, H. *The Catholic Reformation* (1962)

Evennett, H. O., ed. Bossy, J. *The Spirit of the Counter-Reformation* (Cambridge 1968)

Janelle, P. *The Catholic Reformation* (Milwaukee 1949) [P]

Kidd, B. J. *The Counter-Reformation* (1933)

Lucas, H. S. 'Survival of the Catholic Faith in the Sixteenth Century' in *American Catholic Historical Review*, xxix (1943), pp. 25–52

Zeeden, E. W. *Das Zeitalter der Gegenreformation* (Freiburg 1967) [P]

Many aspects are surveyed in vols xvii, xviii of the series, *Histoire de l'Église*, ed. A. Fliche and V. Martin: L. Cristiani, *L'Église à L'Époque du Concile de Trente* (Turin 1948); L. Willaert, *Après le Concile de Trente* (Tournai 1960)

The earlier stages in Germany are well reviewed in J. Lortz, *The Reformation in Germany* (1968), vol. ii.

An invaluable work of reference is the *Dictionnaire de Théologie Catholique*, ed. A. Vacant and others (15 vols, Paris 1903–50); so is *The Oxford Dictionary of the Christian Church*, ed. F. L. Cross (1957)

Boehmer, H. *Ignatius von Loyola* (Stuttgart 1950)

Brodrick, J. *The Origin of the Jesuits* (1940) [P]

Brodrick, J. *The Progress of the Jesuits* (1947)

Brodrick, J. *Saint Peter Canisius* (1935)

Brodrick, J. *Robert Bellarmine* (revised ed., 1961)

Campbell, T. J. *The Jesuits* (2 vols, New York 1921)

Fichter, J. H. *James Laynez, Jesuit* (St. Louis and London 1946)

Fülöp-Miller, R. *The Power and Secret of the Jesuits* (1957)

Garstein, O. *Rome and the Counter-Reformation in Scandinavia* (Copenhagen, Stockholm, Gothenberg 1963)

Martindale, C. C. *The Vocation of Aloysius Gonzaga* (1927)

Rahner, H. *The Spirituality of St. Ignatius Loyola* (Westminster, Maryland 1953)

Smith, G. *Jesuit Thinkers of the Renaissance* (Milwaukee 1939)

OTHER RELIGIOUS LEADERS, ORDERS AND MOVEMENTS

A succinct but well-referenced account of the new Orders will be found in B. J. Kidd, above; a good summary is that by H. O. Evennett in *New Cambridge Modern History*, vol. II, ch. IX.

Auclair, M. *St. Teresa of Ávila* (1953)

Axters, S. *The Spirituality of the Old Low Countries* (1954)

Bainton, R. H. *Bernardino Ochino, Esule e Reformatore Senese . . .* 1487–1563 (Florence 1940)

Blosius, L. *A Book of Spiritual Instruction* (revised ed. 1955)

Bremond, H. *A Literary History of Religious Thought in France* (2 vols, 1928, 1930)

Bruggeman, E. *Les Mystiques Flamands et le Renouveau Catholique Français* (Lille 1928)

Cambridge History of Poland (Cambridge 1950)

Caraman, P. *St. Angela. The Life of Angela Merici Foundress of the Ursulines* (1963)

Cistellini, A. *Figure della Riforma Pretridentino* (Brescia 1948)

Claridge, Mary, *Margaret Clitherow* (1966)

Cohen, J. M. (ed.) *The Life of St. Teresa of Ávila* (1957) [P]

Daniel-Rops, H. *Monsieur Vincent* (1961)

Dicken, E. W. T. *The Crucible of Love* (1963)

Douglas, R. M. *Jacopo Sadoleto* (Cambridge, Mass., 1959)

Graef, H. *The Story of Mysticism* (1966)

Hess, C. *The Capuchins* (New York 1929)

Jedin, H. *Papal Legate at the Council of Trent: Cardinal Seripando* (St Louis and London 1947)

Jouhandeau, M. *St. Philip Neri* (New York 1960)

Kunkel, P. A. *The Theatines in the History of the Catholic Reform* (Washington, D.C. 1941)

Latreille, A., Delaruelle, E., Palanque, J-R. *Histoire du Catholicisme en France* (Paris 1960)

Lyell, J. P. R. *Cardinal Ximenes . . . with an account of the Complutensian Polyglot Bible* (1917)

Mascall, E. L. *A Guide to Mount Carmel* (1939)

Peers, E. A. *Studies of the Spanish Mystics* (4 vols, New York 1927–35)

Peers, E. A. *St. John of the Cross and Other Lectures* (1946)

Peers, E. A. *St. Theresa of Jesus and Other Essays* (1953)

Schenk, W. *Reginald Pole, Cardinal of England* (1950)

Stopp, E. (ed.) *St. Francis of Sales, Selected Letters* (1960)

THE PAPACY AND THE COUNCIL OF TRENT

Evennett, H. O. *The Cardinal of Lorraine and the Council of Trent* (Cambridge 1930)

Hughes, P. *The Church in Crisis* (1961)

Jedin, H. *History of the Council of Trent* (2 vols, 1957, 1961)

Jedin, H. *Crisis and Closure of the Council of Trent* (1967) [P]

Pascoe, L. B. 'The Council of Trent and Bible Study' in *Catholic Historical Review*, LII (1967), pp. 18–38

Pastor, L. von, *History of the Popes from the Close of the Middle Ages* (especially vols. VIII–XV, 1908–28)

Ranke, L. von, *History of the Popes* (3 vols, 1878 and later eds.)

Schroeder, H. J. *Canons and Decrees of the Council of Trent* (1941)

HISTORICAL AND INTELLECTUAL BACKGROUND

Abercrombie, N. *The Origins of Jansenism* (Oxford 1936)

Allen, J. W. *A History of Political Thought in the Sixteenth Century* (1928)

Bataillon, M. *Erasme et l'Espagne* (Paris 1937)

Bossy, J. 'The Character of Elizabethan Catholicism' in *Crisis in Europe, 1560–1660*, ed. T. Aston (1965)

Brandi, K. *The Emperor Charles V* (1939) [P 1965]

Braudel, F. *La Méditerranée et le Monde Méditerranéen à l'Époque de Philippe II* (Paris 1949)

Cantimori, D. *Gli Eretici Italiani del Cinquecento* (Florence 1939)

Copleston, F. *A History of Philosophy* (vol. III, pt. 2; New York 1963) [P]

Dickens, A. G. *Reformation and Society in Sixteenth-Century Europe* (1966) [P]

Elliott, J. H. 'The Mental World of Hernan Cortés' in *Transactions of the Royal Historical Society*, 5 series, XVII (1967), pp. 41–58

Elton, G. R. *Renaissance and Reformation* (revised ed. 1968) [P]

Elton, G. R. *Reformation Europe* (1963) [P]

Garin, E. *Italian Humanism* (Oxford 1965)

Giedion, S. *Space, Time and Architecture* (Cambridge, Mass. 1944)

Hall, A. R. *The Scientific Revolution* (1962)

Haskell, F. *Patrons and Painters* (1963)

Hay, D. (ed.) *The Age of the Renaissance* (1967)

Heer, F. *The Intellectual History of Europe* (1966)

Kamen, H. *The Spanish Inquisition* (1965) [P]

Koenigsberger, H. G. 'Decadence or Shift?' in *Transactions of the Royal Historical Society*, 5 series, X (1960), pp. 1–18

Lecler, J. *Toleration and the Reformation* (2 vols, 1960)

Lees-Milne, J. *Baroque in Spain and Portugal* (1960)

Logan, O. M. T. 'Grace and Justification: Some Italian Views of the 16th and 17th Centuries' in *Journal of Ecclesiastical History*, XX (1969)

Lynch, J. 'Philip II and the Papacy' in *Transactions of the Royal Historical Society*, 5 series, XI (1961), pp. 23–42

McGrath, P. *Papists and Puritans under Elizabeth I* (1937)

McNair, P. *Peter Martyr in Italy* (Oxford 1967)

Mattingly, G. *Renaissance Diplomacy* (1955) [P]

Meyer, A. O. *England and the Catholic Church under Elizabeth* (1916; ed. J. Bossy, 1967)

Neale, J. E. *The Age of Catherine de Medici* (1943) [P]

Olin, J. C. (ed.) *Calvin and Sadoleto, A Reformation Debate* (New York 1965) [P]

Parry, J. H. *The Age of Reconnaissance* (1963) [P]

Polman, P. *L'Élément Historique dans la Controverse Religieuse du XVIe Siècle* (Gembloux 1932)

Renaudet, A. *Préréforme et Humanisme à Paris . . . 1494–1517* (Paris, 2nd edn. 1953)

Rowse, A. L. *The England of Elizabeth* (1950)

Strauss, G. 'The Religious Policies of Dukes Wilhelm and Ludwig of Bavaria' in *Church History*, XXVIII (1959), pp. 350–373

Taton, R. (ed.) *The Beginning of Modern Science* (1964)

Thomson, S. Harrison *Europe in Renaissance and Reformation* (New York 1963)

Trevor-Roper, H. R. *Religion, the Reformation and Social Change* (1967)

Trimble, W. R. *The Catholic Laity in Elizabethan England* (Cambridge, Mass. 1964)

Wedgwood, C. V. *The Thirty Years War* (1938) [P]

Wulf, M. de *History of Medieval Philosophy*, vol. II (1938)

LIST OF ILLUSTRATIONS

72 Portrait of Pius IV; Italian engraving, 1559. British Museum. Photo : Freeman

73 Daniele Crespi, portrait of St Charles Borromeo, c. 1626. Church of the Passion, Milan. Photo : Mansell/Alinari

74 Portrait of Alfonso Salmeron; from the 1602 edition of his *Commentarii* . . ., Cologne. British Museum. Photo : Freeman

75 Giovanni della Robbia and Santi Buglioni, *The Works of Mercy* (detail); terracotta frieze, 1525. Ospedale del Ceppo, Pistoia. Photo : Scala

76 Il Domenichino, *Apotheosis of the Virgin*; fresco, early seventeenth century. Chapel of St Januarius, Naples Cathedral. Photo : Rocco Pedicini, Naples

77 Title-page of the *Canons and Decretals* of the Council of Trent, Rome, 1564. British Museum. Photo : Freeman

78 J. Seisenegger, Sermon of the papal nuncio in the Augustinerkirche, Vienna, 1560. Count Harrach Art Gallery, Vienna

79 Medal of the reign of Pius V commemorating the Battle of Lepanto, 1571. British Museum. Photo: Freeman

80 Heading of the Bull excommunicating Elizabeth I. British Museum. Photo : Freeman

81 Portrait of Gregory XIII; papal medal, 1572. Staatliche Museen, Berlin

82 *Te Deum* in the Sistine Chapel celebrating the Massacre of St Bartholomew; engraving, 1572. British Museum. Photo : Freeman

83 Portrait of Henry IV of France (detail); French School, late sixteenth century. Musée de Peinture, Grenoble. Photo : Giraudon

84 Procession of the League in Paris; French School, sixteenth century. Musée Carnavalet, Paris. Photo : Giraudon

85 Sixtus V; bronze bust. Treia Cathedral. Photo : Mansell/Alinari

86 Clement VIII; bronze bust by G. Albenga, 1601. Façade of Ferrara Cathedral. Photo : Mansell/Alinari

87 Portrait of Sixtus V and his achievements; engraving, Rome, 1589. British Museum. Photo: Freeman

88 Portrait of St Peter Canisius; seventeenth-century engraving. British Museum. Photo : Freeman

89 View of the Escorial; anonymous seventeenth-century painting. Escorial, Madrid. Photo : Mas

90 El Greco, *The Dream of Philip II* (detail), c. 1580. Escorial, Madrid

91 Portrait of Emperor Ferdinand II; painting attributed to Frans Pourbus the Younger, 1619. Prado, Madrid. Photo : Mas

92 Plate from a German translation of Las Casas, *Destruction of the Indies*, Cologne, 1599. British Museum. Photo : Freeman

93 Guercino, portrait of St Philip Neri, 1647. S. Maria in Vallicella, Rome. Photo : Scala

94 S. Maria in Vallicella; a papal medal of 1575. British Museum. Photo : Freeman

95 St Teresa of Ávila; painting by Fray Juan de la Miseria, 1576. Convent of the Carmelites, Seville. Photo : Mas

96 El Greco, *The Burial of Count Orgaz*, 1586. Santo Tomé, Toledo

97 Fray Luis de Leon; drawing from Pacheco's *Descripción de Verdaderos Retratos*, 1599. Museo Lazaro, Madrid. Photo : Mas

98 Title-page of *Imago primi sæculi*, Antwerp, 1640. Library of the Historical Institute of Society of Jesus, Rome

99 Bernini, *Ecstasy of St Teresa*, 1644–52. Cornaro Chapel, S. Maria della Vittoria, Rome. Photo : Scala

100 Borromini, the spire of S. Ivo della Sapienza, Rome, 1642–50

101 Façade of S. Andrea della Valle, Rome; engraving, 1600. British Museum. Photo : Freeman

102 Façade of S. Maria in Vallicella, Rome: engraving, 1600. British Museum. Photo : Freeman

103 Interior of the Gesù, Rome; engraving by V. Regnartius, c. 1600. British Museum. Photo: Freeman

104 Emblem of St François de Sales; from A. Gambart, *La Vie symbolique du bienheureux François de Sales*, 1664. British Museum. Photo : Freeman

105 St François de Sales with St Jeanne de Chantal; painting by Noel Hallé. Church of St Louis, Paris. Photo: Giraudon

106 St Vincent de Paul among the Ladies of Charity; French School, eighteenth century Musée de l'Assistance Publique, Paris

107 Louis le Nain, *Beggars at a Doorway*; mid-seventeenth century. Metropolitan Museum of Art, New York. The Metropolitan Museum of Art, Purchase, 1871

108 J. Callot, 'Punishments'; study for *The Miseries of War*, 1633. Photo: Giraudon

109 Georges de la Tour, *St Irene with St Sebastian*. Church of Broglie, Eure

110 Emblem adapted by Francis Quarles and its Jesuit source from H. Hugo, *Pia Desideria* (1629); from Francis Quarles, *Emblemes*, 1635. British Museum. Photo: Freeman

111 J. de Heem, *The Eucharist*, 1648. Kunsthistorisches Museum, Vienna

112 Goya, sketch of a penitent. Prado, Madrid

Page numbers in italics refer to illustrations